Reviews

"This is an eloquently recoun̲ed and heartbreaking story—readers will admire Menara's honesty, although her willingness to describe the most intimate details of her caregiving duties may prove too frank for some tastes. Illustrated with family photographs throughout, the memoir closes with an unexpected revelation and offers a message of hope and healing that will be of value to others who have faced similar circumstances."

— *Kirkus Reviews*
(starred review)

A powerful read . . . Wendy's turbulent childhood is packed with joyful moments and her relationships with those around her are lively and dynamic; but she also faces sorrow and tragedy in equal measure.

Silence of Shame also teaches lessons about living with disease . . . Wendy doesn't leave anything out of this unflinching memoir, and her attempt to leave no stone unturned and reveal all the shame and stigma her family faced pays off. There were moments that made me laugh and cry, and I will definitely be re-reading this again in the future.

—*Madison Butz,*
Development Manager,
National Multiple Sclerosis Society

I highly recommend reading this memoir to understand the bonds of a family, even in the worst of times, and to also provide courage to anyone suffering similarly, that life can take a turn for the better.

All families have secrets and deal with them in a variety of ways. Some go to the graves with those who have hidden them, while others bubble to the top in ways that can't be avoided. To find the courage to absorb these secrets, process them, and apply them to our lives—hopefully in a positive way—is a blessing.

I applaud Wendy for her bravery in putting her memories to paper, so others may find comfort in knowing they aren't alone and there is a path to acceptance and forgiveness.

—*Linda Palmer*
Director/Producer, Runaway Films

The life experiences and living conditions the author faced as a very young child and while growing up touched me in a way that hurt my heart . . . The responsibilities and chores required of her in caring for her bedridden mother are like no other child of that age in my knowledge or experience. In reading this memoir the author appeared to have far more maturity than the average five-to-seven-year-old child. To live with the knowledge that her mother was dying and to have that death occur just as she entered her teen years is heartbreaking and inconceivable.

This book is sometimes difficult to read, as well as being at times heartwarming, joyful, and hopeful. It is truly a book worth reading.

—*Mardel Taguinod*
Retired Pre-school, Kindergarten, and
First Grade School Teacher
Fairfield-Suisun Unified School District

TREES
Joyce Kilmer—1886–1918

I think that I shall never see
A poem lovely as a tree.
A tree whose hungry mouth is prest
Against the sweet earth's flowing breast;
A tree that looks at God all day,
And lifts her leafy arms to pray;
A tree that may in summer wear
A nest of robins in her hair;
Upon whose bosom snow has lain;
Who intimately lives with rain.
Poems are made by fools like me,
But only God can make a tree.

Silence
of Shame

A Child Caring for Her
Bedridden Mother

Wendy J. Menara

Turtle Mountain Stories

Wendy J. Menara
P.O. Box 6652
Vacaville, CA 95696
wendyjmenara@gmail.com
www.wendyjmenara.com

Printed in the United States of America
Book Designer, Jim Shubin, www.bookalchemist.net
Editor, Jean Mansen, www.jeanmansen.com
Line Editing/Proofreading by Arnetta Jackson,
    www.lineuponlineservices.com

This book reflects the author's recollection of events. Some names have been changed to protect the privacy of those depicted. Dialogue has been recreated from memory.

A portion of proceeds from this book will go to the National Multiple Sclerosis Society. To learn more and donate visit www.nationalmssociety.org.

Publisher's Cataloging-in-Publication Data

Names: Menara, Wendy J., author.
Title: Silence of shame : a child caring for her bedridden mother, a childhood memoir / by Wendy J. Menara.
Description: Vacaville, CA; Wendy J. Menara, 2020.
Identifiers: ISBN: 978-1-7353969-0-3 (pbk.)
| 978-1-7353969-1-0 (e-book) 978-1-7353969-2-7 hb.)
Subjects: LCSH Menara, Wendy J.–Childhood and youth. | Multiple sclerosis–Patients. | Multiple sclerosis–Patients–Family relationships. | Mothers and daughters. | People with disabilities–Family relationships. | People with disabilities–Biography. | Abused children–United States–Biography. | Michigan–Biography. | BISAC BIOGRAPHY & AUTOBIOGRAPHY / Personal Memoirs
Classification: LCC RC377 .M456 2020 | DDC 616.8/34/092--dc23

ISBN 978-1-7353969-0-3 Print PaperBack
ISBN 978-1-7353969-1-0 (e-Book)
ISBN 978-1-7353969-2-7 (Hardback)

Dedication

~ Greg ~
Oh, dear brother, so many years ago it was only our
imaginations that spurred us forth to believe in a world
greater than the one we saw with our physical eyes.

~ Bill and Ang ~
providing a foundation

~ Jean ~
encouraging me with kindness

~ Charlene ~
inspiring friendship

Contents

We Choose Our Joys and Sorrows
Long Before We Experience Them

Khalil Gibran

Preface

My fear of betraying our tightly held family secrets and sharing them with strangers was daunting. My mantra throughout the writing of this memoir—Embrace Your Story. Own Your Voice. Sharing intimate family truths was overwhelming and, at times, left me grappling with self-doubt. My mother didn't broadcast her safeguarded secrets for a reason; why should I reveal them and provide fertile life to long ago memories in the writing of this book?

But distinguished author Anne Lamott's quote helped me forge ahead: "You own everything that happened to you. Tell your stories." That sentiment propelled me to convey my narrative as honestly as I could so I could find my voice and strip those secrets of any last power they may have had over me.

I felt compelled to share this unique story of caring for a bedridden mother diagnosed with multiple sclerosis (MS). The caregiving that my mother received from her children in the 1970s would not happen in today's society. Today's rules and cultural norms are different. The challenges our family faced in a single-parent household with a mother who could be particularly cruel would not be permitted to exist in this day and age.

I investigated different angles to gather information. Gogebic County Courthouse public records provided insight. In the early-to-mid-twentieth century, local newspapers (especially those in smaller towns) shared quite a bit of information about local events and people. Newspapers.com aided in much of my research.

The title of this memoir changed as I wrote. The original working title was "Moments in Time," which is what this book is: episodes of what life was like as a child caring for an incapacitated mother. I don't remember everything. But I remember enough. In the writing of my childhood memoir, I observed that as I put pen to paper, additional experiences tucked away deep in the far corners of my psyche surfaced.

As memories returned, I realized that now, as an adult, those past distressing experiences couldn't harm me the way I once believed they had the power to do. This newfound insight allowed me the courage to relive the harsh circumstances of my childhood that I had stashed in the far depths of my mind. In addition, I came to fully comprehend that as human beings, we all hang in the balance of light and darkness. As heartless as my mother was, she could also be a loving, kind mother who I believe did the best with what she had. Our entire family did the best that we could.

In addition to grappling with oppressive childhood experiences, I recognized that the death of my mother when I was an adolescent was overwhelming. I persevered after her death, but didn't get a chance to fully grieve or process the loss. During the exploration of my childhood within these pages, I questioned what survival mechanism kicks in that spurs us forth to 'soldier onward.' I realized how children find their unique ways to cope when they lose a parent.

By sharing my childhood story and subsequent scars and vulnerabilities, I hope that anyone who cares for a loved one with a chronic illness, has weathered a childhood fraught with abuse of any kind, feels ashamed of secrets that weigh heavily on their heart, or lost a parent while in their youth will know that there are healthy ways of coping. No matter the weight of despair, we are not alone. It is possible to find understanding, acceptance, and peace.

There shall be roads I will never travel
Mountains I shall never climb
Oceans I shall never set sail upon
And still I find peace

Wendy J. Menara

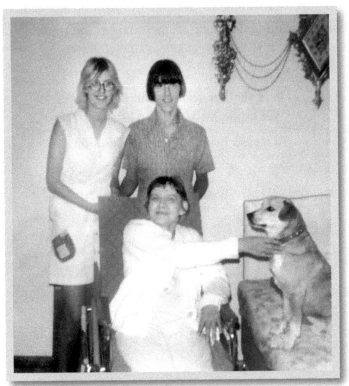

My mother, aka Mumma (Shirley Ann Menara), in her
orange wheelchair, nine months before she passed away
at the age of 46. Prior to the wheelchair, she had been
confined to her bed for about eight years. Alongside her
are my siblings, Madeline and Greg, and our beloved
dog, Peppy. Summer of 1976.

The Orange Wheelchair

For as long as I can remember, Mumma yearned to experience the fresh air and sunshine on her body. The daily routine of her children completing the normal household chores of cooking, cleaning, grocery shopping, and laundry, in addition to her personal grooming, bathing, feeding, and giving her the bedpan must have burdened her heart and soul. This proud Chippewa- and Irish-blooded woman must have had dreams and desires of her own, but somewhere along the way, her journey ended up in a tiny, two-bedroom, tin-roofed house caring for six of her ten children in a once thriving, Midwestern mining town.

In the 1960s and 1970s information about MS was limited. The doctor always told Mumma she would die from the disease. Mumma had no reason not to believe him. Her inevitable death was a normal conversation in our household. It wasn't a matter of 'if' she would die, it was only a matter of 'when' she would die.

Family conversations often included who would get the dishes, knick-knacks, pictures that hung on the wall, family photos, or her wedding ring. And, more importantly, the question of exactly when she would die wore heavily on our young hearts. She assured us that she wouldn't leave until we were old enough to take care of ourselves.

In 1976, when I was twelve years old, the family received fabulous news that involved us taking a long trip to a big hospital in Minneapolis. This was a milestone trip: Mumma might get some help for her MS. This trip also allowed her freedom from the confines of the house. As the attendants carried her meager, frail body out to the waiting van, she quickly lifted her eyes toward the blue sky—and then just as quickly, lowered her head. Those same hazel-brown eyes that could stare you down if you ever thought of misbehaving couldn't handle the influx of outside sunlight that she had been denied for so many years.

Her dark hair hung over her optimistic face as they carried her on the stretcher to the van. She occasionally glanced up to the heavens as if searching for something far more significant than my child-self could understand. Yet, even at my young age, I saw the vulnerability in my mother. She was mortal.

While we waited for Mumma, we played and explored in the enormous hospital. I was mesmerized by the glass-enclosed skyway. I imagined what would happen if the glass broke and I fell atop the fast-moving cars below. I scampered off and found the escalators to be a far greater form of entertainment.

At the end of a long day, when the doctor explained to Mumma that they could not cure her MS, I was devastated. These were important doctors at a big city hospital; surely, they could do something. But it was not to be. Mumma kept a brave face, but I knew she was heartbroken. We all were. In place of a cure, they offered relief in the form of a donated wheelchair. It had an orange leather seat and backrest and silver handles. It didn't matter that it was chipped in places or that the orange leather was peeling;

this burly wheeled contraption served its purpose—mobility, and some temporary relief for her otherwise restricted existence.

Back home, the attendants lifted her body onto the tattered orange seat. Her paralyzed left hand lay limp as she tolerated the attendant who was trying to position her more comfortably. She struggled to situate herself with her unimpaired right hand and then, finally, she allowed the full weight of her body to settle against the worn backrest of the wheelchair. Her eyes lit up like the noonday sun. That spark came from deep within her shackled soul and emanated across the room. She was proud of her accomplishment, and we were proud of her! A window had been thrust open that up until that moment was sealed shut. My mother was free from the confines of her bed. She was mobile. It was a welcome, hopeful beginning for our mother.

The hope didn't last long. Initially, we lifted her into the wheelchair, but she couldn't last for more than an hour or two in the upright position. It hurt her body. I suppose the many years of a bedridden existence caused her muscles to atrophy.

Over a short time, the orange wheelchair was used less and less. When we were bored, and Mumma slept, my siblings and I took turns pushing each other to see how fast we could spin in circles. In time, the orange wheelchair sat vacant in a corner, collecting dust. Mumma found refuge on the dark-green couch in the living room. From that point on, things quickly went downhill.

Within that year, Mumma's health spiraled downward with dementia and then cervical cancer. We children could no longer care for her and she was admitted to Gogebic County Hospital. We spent a good deal of time in that building. One day while visiting her after school, I picked up her bone-thin body to give her the bedpan. Her backside was saddled with bedsores; the stench was unbearable. In one section the flesh was stripped to the bone. I bit my lip and suppressed my anguish. "Mumma, are you okay? Can you hear me?" But she was too despondent in her morphine state to offer any response. I saw the light fading in her eyes. The fight was over. She had lost the battle.

Shortly after that visit, she died from a heart attack. She was forty-six years old. I suppose that in the end, it was just too much for her. It was her time to move on. Surely, Mumma wouldn't have left unless she knew I was old enough to take care of myself. I would make her proud. I was ready to face the world. I was thirteen years old.

❧ ❧ ❧

More than forty years have passed since my mother's death. I unraveled questions that I had long ago set aside. Being older and stronger now, I share my journey in this collection of memories as a child caregiver.

Shirley, in her vibrant days, sits atop a late '40s Plymouth in Marenisco, Michigan, where she grew up, circa early 1950s.

Tan Shoes and a Walker

The Beginning Years

My older sister Madeline and I were jumping back and forth between the double bed and the twin-size rollaway bed. We danced wildly while listening to the Beatle's song, "A Hard Day's Night." While my sister bounced on one bed, the rollaway was my dance floor.

In midair, I flung the sky-blue, plastic curtains and watched them billow as they lightly cascaded down the peeling aqua walls. As I spun around, my eye captured the orange-and-yellow label of the 45-rpm record as it spun 'round and 'round on the record player.

I heard Mumma holler, but the music had transported me to a happier world. I couldn't care less about Mumma's yelling. I leaped onto the nearby double bed, exchanging places with my sister. Then, the yardstick's crack against the wall snapped me out of my fantasy.

We stopped dead in our tracks. I braced myself against the curved, back bedroom wall and fixated on Mumma gripping tightly to her walker as she shuffled steadily toward us. Clearly, she was not happy. Mumma was all business with a yardstick clutched in one hand as she haltingly dragged her feet on the dark wooden floor. My eyes zeroed in on her crippled foot, knowing she couldn't catch me. I hopped off the bed and bolted past her as the wooden yardstick grazed my thighs. I crouched under the kitchen table and grasped the curved aluminum legs. But

Madeline wasn't so lucky. She took a yardstick lashing for both of us that day. It's the only memory I have of my mother walking.

Yet, even as a child, I figured Mumma couldn't have always been this way—she must have skipped, run, and danced at one time.

While writing this memoir, I unearthed a photo of my mother sitting on the outside steps of our house at 308 West McLeod Street wearing her tan shoes. She looks frail in this photo, just a fraction of the vibrant and dazzling woman she once appeared to be in earlier pictures. According to newspaper research, my mother was admitted to Grandview Hospital in April 1965 for the first time, where she stayed for one month while the doctors tried to figure out what was wrong with her. It was the mid-1960s and there wasn't a lot of information about MS in those days.

The doctors at the hospital determined that orthopedic shoes would offer support, the medicine would ease the pain, and the walker would compensate for her instability. She maintained her mobility for a few years, but by the age of thirty-six, my mother was completely bedridden. I was four years old.

Even though I wasn't tall enough to help my mother much, I assisted when I could. I brought her water and coffee, gave her sponge baths, and curled her hair. At the beginning of her bedridden condition, she still liked to style her hair. I nestled up behind her head, combed her fine black hair, and gently twirled the pink plastic curlers in place. On special occasions, she even wore lipstick, especially if we had company.

I also helped her put on her chalky-white ankle socks and her tan shoes. I enjoyed tying her shoelaces, as it gave me a chance to practice learning how to tie bows. After carefully folding the ankle socks and securing the shoelaces, Mumma gazed at her feet and wiggled them. She smiled and told me what a good job I did. I asked her if she would ever walk again, and she took a long drag from her cigarette, exhaled, and shrugged, "I don't know, Wendy. I hope so."

She didn't get better. As the disease progressed, Mumma stopped using the walker and wearing the tan shoes altogether. Once, I slipped into those tan shoes and tried to walk in them, but they were too large for me, even after tying the shoelaces extra tight. Her walker became my small-scale jungle gym. When Mumma slept, I dragged her walker into the bedroom and pushed it next to the bed and hung on it upside down.

Those tan shoes—they sat in the closet for years. One day, years later, my sister and I were cleaning and purging things at our mother's request. Madeline came out of the bedroom holding up the shoes and said, "What about these? What do you wanna do with them?" Mumma scanned the shoes in disgust, smashed out her cigarette, and said, "Throw 'em in the garbage." It was then I knew my mother would never walk again.

At the time of this photo, Shirley had been diagnosed with multiple sclerosis, but was somewhat mobile and enjoyed a day outside wearing her tan shoes, circa late 1960s.

Glen Morrison (Gramps), Shirley, Josephine Morrison (Grandma). Across the street is the old Marenisco Town Hall, circa 1950s.

Where Did She Go?

From 1965 through 1967, while my mother was admitted for prolonged hospital stays, my brother Kelly, who was one year younger, and I stayed with our grandparents in Marenisco, a nearby town. While living with my grandparents I created a strong emotional bond with them. My grandfather, Glen, worked at the local lumber yard, and my grandmother, Josephine, was a homemaker. I loved them dearly, and though I was only a very young child, I have vivid memories of special moments spent with them.

Despite my grandfather's inability to hear or speak, he was a gregarious, social man, and everyone in town adored him. He was known as Gramps or Bobbie. To talk with him, you had to learn sign language, and kids and adults did this to spend quality time with him. Gramps was born in Idaho and often showed me photos of the majestic mountains and winding Snake River. My favorite game with Gramps was 'horsey.' I jumped on his back and we galloped around the living room. Or sometimes he tossed me up in the air and then caught me. The tickly feeling in my stomach and the air rushing over my skin delighted my toddler body.

Though I cherished my fun-loving grandfather, I had a deep spiritual connection with my grandmother. Unlike Gramps, Grandma was quiet and reserved. She had gray hair and a pouch belly. She was slightly bent over at the waist, and it hurt for her to carry me.

Grandma loved to garden. As a child, it appeared to me that her garden was a forest of tall flowers and shrubs. Purple and yellow flowers towered over my tiny body as I reached for the petals as they danced in the wind. While she worked in the garden, I frolicked between the lofty flowers and chased the monarch butterflies.

My grandparents' house was across the street from the Town Hall, which was surrounded by a spacious, grassy public area. It had a wonderful play area, including a merry-go-round, where my grandfather let me play. I slept in a bedroom under an open window and loved the purring sounds of the lawn mower I heard in the distance and the smell of freshly cut grass. Many a time I was lulled to sleep by that sound and smell.

Etched in my memory, too, was sitting at the kitchen table while Grandma made Cream of Wheat. I sat patiently, attentive to my grandmother as she stirred the spoon in the ancient pot. I reminded her that I liked my Cream of Wheat lumpy. Grandma nodded and smiled, then carried the pan to the kitchen table and spooned out a hearty serving in my cereal bowl. I poured a mountain of sugar atop the porridge, smooshed everything down with my spoon, and watched the whole mess dissolve into the milk.

But those golden moments passed. One evening, I peered into the bathroom and saw my invincible grandmother hunched over the bathtub. I didn't understand what she was doing and why she was making that loud, gagging sound. She sluggishly turned to me and managed that kind smile of hers. She jolted her head toward the tub and shooed me away. But I didn't move. I just stood there fixated on my grandmother's body and what looked to me like silver beads spewing out of her mouth. As an adult, I learned that this silvery substance was attributed to kidney failure. She stood up and stumbled into the bedroom. I cautiously approached the tub and peered over the side. It was filled with a silvery, gooey, bead-like substance. Even at four years of age, I knew something was wrong.

Time moved slowly. It was the dead of winter, January 1968, when my grandmother died. Snow was as high as the street signs. I was riding home from the funeral with my great-aunt Ruthie, whom we always called 'Aunt Ruthie.' She was my grandmother's sister, a gentle woman with dark hair like my mother's. I sat in the back seat of the car and demanded to know where Grandma went. Aunt Ruthie said, "Your grandmother is in heaven." My aunt's answer didn't make sense in my child mind. Instead, I turned my attention out past the car window to the ominous white landscape. I was upset and growing more so.

When we arrived at my house, I was still muttering to myself asking, "Where's Grandma?" I pushed my way through the weathered, mud-colored, front door and made a right turn into our cramped kitchen, while Aunt Ruthie took a left turn to visit my mother in the living room. I stood under the kitchen window, tucked behind the yellow kitchen table. The rage of losing my grandma and not knowing where she went consumed me.

I found myself repeating "Where is she? Where'd she go?" Growing increasingly agitated, my four-year-old body began to tremble; then a high-pitched, ear-piercing sound overwhelmed me. My eyes riveted on a drinking glass when all of a sudden—the glass toppled over and rolled next to the soap dish. The thing is—I wasn't touching it. I was directing the item's movement from my mind. As I continued in this spellbound trance, a few dishes fell into the sink. I felt hot and the room was spinning. No longer chanting, "Where did she go?" I now zeroed in on the bottom drawer of the stove. The more I stared, the more anger built up inside me. Then all of a sudden, the bottom drawer of the stove popped open. A few pots and pans flew out and smashed into the fridge. Aunt Ruthie rushed into the kitchen. Her eyes were wide with fear. I peered up helplessly at my aunt, while Mumma was yelling from the next room. I knew I was causing this commotion, but I couldn't stop it.

Years later, I learned that this episode was a psychic occurrence known as telekinesis. During this chaotic happening, however, I had no idea what was causing all this frenzy. I braced myself against the kitchen wall and Aunt Ruthie grabbed my shoulders. Upon her touch, the pandemonium of toppled kitchen items came to an abrupt halt. The high-pitched noise in my head ceased, and I stopped shaking. My aunt quickly shuffled me out of the kitchen. Mumma demanded to know what happened. Instead, I ran to the bedroom and buried myself under the bed covers. This episode frightened me greatly, and I never had this type of experience ever again.

After Grandma's passing, Grandpa decided to move closer to us. He found a decent-sized apartment for himself near our house. During this transition, we went back to Marenisco to pack and sort through items. As people mingled, I went to Grandma's closet. It seemed like a forest of clothes surrounding and encircling me. I mingled in and out of the clothes, rubbing my hands and face across all the fabrics, taking in every texture, every smell. The scent of Emeraude perfume comforted me. I came across her gray mink stole and buried my face into the luxurious mane. I noticed her favorite stylish, blue-colored broach, unpinned it from her dress, and joyfully wore it. I slept with that ornamental pin under my pillow for a number of years.

I had secret visits with Grandma. I never told a soul for fear that no one would believe me. I had a distinct ringing in my ears on the initial mystical visit. The noise frightened me. When it finally stopped, I opened my eyes, and there was my grandmother. I shook my head to make the vision stop. But it didn't. She smiled. My body grew warm and the fear subsided. I knew she had died, yet in these visits, she was very much alive to me. I felt tingly inside. Her presence was overwhelmingly that of love. Her smile was as warm as it was when I lived with her.

She had a golden glow about her and she whispered to me. I do not recollect what those words were, yet I appreciated our private chats in those beginning years following her death. From that point forward, I figured out when Grandma was about to 'visit' because I heard that distinct ringing. Eventually, as time passed, her visits became less frequent until the visits stopped altogether.

Though we were Catholic, our family didn't talk a lot about God or Jesus, but we did have a large, thick Bible with a padded, white cover that had pictures throughout. Some of the pictures were images of heaven. One picture, in particular, captured my imagination. A man surrounded by billowy white clouds ascended a stairway leading him toward a golden mansion. Halfway up the stairs, Jesus stood with his hand outreached, welcoming the person into his heavenly home. I spent hours nestled on the bed holding the Bible and studying this image.

I pretended that this person was my grandmother walking those stairs to her home in the clouds. This image offered me peace. Despite the fact no one could ever fully answer where Grandma went, the idea of her walking the stairs into heaven consoled me.

I lived with my grandparents for a short time only. Yet, the time with my grandmother was long enough that we formed a solid psychic bond and I was spiritually and emotionally devastated when she passed. Her death was a life-defining moment.

❦ ❦ ❦

Because of my early experiences with the death of both my mother and grandmother, I had a deep interest in what lies beyond this natural world. As a young adult I studied metaphysical and clairvoyant topics. I gained greater insight into what happens to persons when they pass over; for instance, as a spirit we are eternal. Although our body may expire, our soul essence continues on in the afterlife. I wholeheartedly plan on meeting my grandmother and mother on the other side.

I also learned that, though telekinesis is a rare phenomenon, people do have these abilities. I trust my childhood telekinetic event resulted from the confusion and fear of not having a clear picture of where my grandmother went. The anger (energy) built up around me, and the frustration grew in the car, so by the time I entered the kitchen, I let loose. Yes, I had a Carrie (the girl with supernatural powers in Stephen King's horror novel) moment—with no blood, thankfully!

Wendy Menara. When my mother was initially diagnosed with multiple sclerosis, my younger brother and I lived with our grandparents in Marenisco, Michigan. Here I am in front of my grandparents' house, circa 1967.

Family Shuffle

After my grandmother died in early 1968, the caregiving that my mother relied upon no longer existed. My mother was now permanently bedridden, and Social Services thought it appropriate—barring any harm—to have the three daughters live with their mother and, consequently, act as caregivers. Thus, our family shuffle began.

I was the second youngest of the ten children in our family. Mumma and Dad married in 1949 and divorced in the early 1960s. At the time of the divorce, the children were split between my mother and father. Kelly and I lived with Mumma in Ironwood. The other children resided with my dad in Bessemer, a neighboring town.

Debbie, who was the oldest of the three girls, was the first to make the move to Ironwood. She was only in the sixth grade, but Social Services was determined to keep the three sisters together with their ailing mother.

Debbie revealed years later that, because of the contested divorce proceedings, she had to go to court and be interviewed by the judge. Even though the move was difficult for her, since she liked living in Bessemer, she proved to the Courts that she was a responsible young daughter. It wasn't long after that Madeline also came to live with us full time. My brothers remained with my dad but often visited us in Ironwood.

Once Debbie joined the household, I was eager to go to school like her. Being an August child meant I was too young for kindergarten but could enroll in Head Start. It was a government program recently developed in the mid-sixties to serve low-income children and their families. I repeatedly begged my mother, "When can I go?" I desperately desired to join the ranks of my other siblings who went to school. While Mumma kept a brave face, I wonder if she was facing the inevitable—her children were growing up.

My first day of Head Start at Central School was exciting. The evening before, I meticulously polished my black-and-white saddle shoes, scrubbed my shoelaces, and picked out my favorite moss-green, gold, and brown checkered dress. Though I was sad about leaving Mumma alone, the exhilaration when the bus pulled up overrode any concerns I had about my mother. I sprinted out of the house, across the huge front lawn, and proudly boarded the bus.

But that first week proved traumatic. Mrs. Gregory, our Head Start teacher, was steely. During our morning bathroom break, I was washing my hands when I heard screams coming from outside the girls' restroom. I, along with the other girls, dashed out horrified to witness Mrs. Gregory across the hallway holding up our classmate by his ear right in front of the classroom door. His feet were literally dangling off the floor as she scolded him. Huddled together, we were frozen in fear. The boy's screams echoed in the vast corridor as he struggled to free himself. Our teacher eventually released him and then shouted at us to return to the classroom.

I was petrified and figured quickly that I had better behave while in school or the same painful fate could happen to me. Fear was instilled in me at an early age, both in school and at home; at times, Mumma could be merciless. She managed to control us and devised techniques to discipline us from the confines of her bed.

The punishment that had the greatest and lasting impact on me happened when I was around five or six years old. I did something 'bad.' I don't recall what terrible trespass I committed; but what was imprinted on my subconscious was the aftermath of my wrongdoing. Mumma was angry. So angry the only way she could teach me a lesson was to ignore me. Initially, I assumed her silent treatment would pass; but it didn't. I stood near the front door within range of the green couch and asked her a question. She deliberately ignored me and turned to my sister Madeline and asked her a question. I was confused—did Mumma not hear me? I asked the question again, but this time she smirked. Her lip snarled. She diverted her piercing hazel eyes in the other direction. Her eye color could change depending on her mood—at times, brown and at other times, green. She was livid. Panic-stricken, I thought to myself—she is doing this on purpose!

I broke out in tears and approached the green couch where she was stationed and begged for her to talk to me. "Mumma, please!" She waved me off with her hand and asked Madeline to give her a cigarette. I stood there despondent, trying to digest what was happening. I don't remember how long she deliberately snubbed me, but it was plenty of time and the rejection was daunting.

I stomped my feet, "Mumma, please talk to me. I'm sorry." She proceeded to stare right through me as if I was invisible. The silent treatment was deafening. The punishment was an eternity. I bolted from the living room into the bedroom. I grabbed my doll, Marella, slid under the bedcovers, and cried myself to sleep.

Little did she know—or perhaps she did—she broke me that evening. I learned my lesson: do not make Mumma angry or she will withhold love. Her denial of affection that evening was earth-shattering. From that point forward, I did all that I could to not provoke her. I needed her to love me, and I wanted her to be proud of me.

In first grade I decided to walk home from school. I thought it would please my mother to know how confident and independent I was. I dashed down the hallway, passed the principal's office, leaped down the stairs, and pushed open the doors of Central School to a bright, sunny spring afternoon.

Only snippets of the one-mile journey home remain: melted snow on the ground; squinting my eyes as I glanced up at the bright sun; one woman peering down at me; my intent focus on the crosswalk light waiting for it to change color; sauntering past Carlson's Supermarket.

But my plan didn't turn out as I'd hoped. Mumma was upset. After getting reprimanded, I was sent to bed without supper—my independent spirit crushed. I didn't do that again.

Once I settled into my school routine, there were moments when I found myself gazing through the classroom windows, wondering how Mumma was doing at home. I figured she was listening to her favorite radio station,

WJMS, or watching TV, but besides that—how did Mumma feel about being home alone? What did she think about all day? Was she afraid, bored, lonely? What if she couldn't reach the bedpan? What if it spilled while she was trying to remove it?

The weekday morning routine continued, until one day—my siblings and I sauntered in through the front door after school, and Mumma was lying in a fetal position on the green couch—a look of terror plastered on her face. Tears flowed as she relayed the frightening story. At some point during the day, a giant, speckled spider made an appearance. Helpless, she kept an eye on the arachnid as it crawled its way steadily along the wall toward the green sofa.

As the eight-legged creature inched closer to the couch, she smashed it with her peanut butter sandwich. This event shook Mumma to the core. It was the first occurrence that I witnessed my mother both frightened and vulnerable. Things would change after that.

Mr. Wilson was one of our social workers. He was a kind-hearted man, and his easygoing nature comforted me. As proud as Mumma was, she knew we needed additional help. Mr. Wilson assured Mumma that he would find someone to help our family while we were in school.

A short, perky, feisty woman with red hair and a summery smile named Agnes showed up. She was a smoker—like Mumma. She came to our house three days a week to cook and clean. I wasn't sure about Agnes until she set a plate of chicken and dumplings in front of me. That woman could cook. Her vivacious nature and a high-spirited laugh flooded our dwelling with warmth and exuberance. I always looked forward to seeing Agnes when I came home from school. She told me a funny story or asked me how my day went. She made me feel special.

Even though Mumma sometimes complained that Agnes was too loud, I had the sense she appreciated her. Day in and day out of a bedridden existence can exert a toll on any individual, and for Mumma, having someone to talk to when she was home alone all day must have eased her loneliness.

Wendy with her two older sisters, Madeline and Debbie. My sisters and I enjoy a Midwestern summer day on the porch of our Quonset hut on McLeod Street, Ironwood, Michigan, circa Summer 1969.

The Bedpan and the TV Tray

By the start of first grade, I had the enemas and bedpan delivery down to a science.

We all took turns giving Mumma the bedpan, but she preferred the girls to give it to her if possible. It made her especially uncomfortable asking my brothers, so it was my sisters' and my primary responsibility. The bedpan was shiny and silver. It was a delicate balance of using one arm to help lift her hips in the air and using the other arm to glide the bedpan under her buttocks. Thankfully, Mumma was a lightweight woman. The tricky part was getting the filled bedpan out from underneath her body without spilling the contents. It could be exceptionally messy. As a result, I learned the art of bedpan withdrawal, or suffered the splash of urine along with a furrowed brow from Mumma.

In the winter months, the bedpan was icy-cold in my hands and a sharp contrast to the warm swirling yellow urine as I gingerly carried it to the bathroom and emptied the astringent waste.

The first time I saw blood, I was frightened. "Mumma, there's blood?" She dismissively remarked, "It's what women do. Go get some towels." I scampered off to the hallway, grabbed a towel off the shelf, returned, and laid it on the bed while she thrust her hips into the air.

When I first assisted Mumma with her Kotex belt and pads, it was challenging for her and for me. She was both uncomfortable and embarrassed while explaining how to hook the dangly contraption around her lower body as I struggled to figure the difference between the front and back sides of the white stretchy bands. First, there was an elastic belt I had to fasten around her hips. The belt also had miniature clips with loops dangling in the front and back. Then there was a super long maxi-pad with long, white tags. I was expected to slip the ends of the pad into these tiny openings. It wasn't the easiest of tasks as I hunched over my mother atop the bed doing my utmost to maneuver the belt, loops, and pad. I can only imagine how embarrassed she must've been, too, having her daughter's hands all up in her private parts.

As any dutiful daughter would do—after that initial unsuccessful incident—one day I snuck the belt and a clean pad, tucked them under my shirt, and pranced into the bathroom. I shut the door behind me, locked it, took my seat atop the rim of the bathtub, and practiced looping the maxi-pad into the itty-bitty openings. I wanted to be primed and ready to tackle this task with ease the next time Mumma had her period.

Quite often, Mumma was constipated. Looking back, I presume it was all the medications that restricted her bowel movements. In the 1960s and '70s, however, the side effects of all the pills she ingested were never addressed. We gave her enemas to help alleviate the stress she endured. We started with a hot washrag held over her backside and, if that was unsuccessful, we pulled out the red-colored hot-water bottle. It took trial and error on our part to get the water temperature just right.

On one occasion, the water was too hot, and Mumma bellowed in anguish when the scalding water was injected into her rectum. I never did that again. From that point forward, I obsessively checked the temperature on my wrist or with my pinky finger. If an enema didn't do the job, one of us was sent to the store to pick up prune juice or Ex-Lax. We quickly figured out just how messy ingesting that chocolate substance could be when confined to a bed and your daughters don't get the bedpan perched under your bum in time.

The TV tray was an integral piece of furniture in our house. It was where all of Mumma's critical items were kept—cigarettes, pill bottles, ashtray, and her cup of coffee. Each item had its own strategic spot, fitting together just so; otherwise, there wouldn't have been space to stow the items she required to get through the day while we were at school. Tucked under the TV tray was the sturdy, chocolate-colored piano bench. We routinely put the bedpan under the couch, but before leaving each morning, we placed the bedpan on the piano bench.

In the beginning years, one of her hands was stable enough that she could use the bedpan by herself while we were gone for the day. After she was done using it, she placed the bedpan back on the bench and covered it with a towel or newspaper.

In time, her hand weakened, so it became increasingly difficult for her to pull out the bedpan in a timely manner. Upon arriving home after school, it was not uncommon to witness Mumma engrossed in her TV show, "Dark

Shadows," as she lingered in urine-drenched sheets and clothes because she had spilled the contents of the bedpan. We started laying towels under her every morning as a precaution. Eventually, Mumma stopped wearing regular tops and resorted to hospital gowns. It made bathing smoother for her and for us.

Growing up with a bedridden mother was what I was accustomed to. Giving her the bedpan, enemas, changing her Kotex, shaving her legs, cutting her nails, massaging her feet, rubbing Bengay on her aching muscles, giving her sponge baths, washing and combing her hair was routine. That was my childhood.

Wendy, two years old, and Shirley. Behind us to the right
is my favorite lilac bush along with a myriad of trees I
climbed as a child. July 1965.

I Called Her Mumma

It wasn't mom, ma, mamma—it was Mumma with a short sounding u. I'm not sure why we called her that—we just did. I didn't think anything of it. It was recess time at Central School, and we were on the playground atop a mammoth snow hill. Hundreds of inches of snow fell each winter, so it was common to sled down snowplowed embankments, create snow forts, or participate in snowball fights—wintertime entertainment in the upper regions of our country. On this remarkably frigid, wintery day, a few of us were making a snowman and quibbling if the snow-man should wear a scarf. No one wanted to volunteer his or her scarf. I argued, "A snowman needs a scarf. Mumma always makes me wear one." One kid chuckled. I raised an eyebrow, "What?" The kinder classmate chimed in, "I have to wear a scarf, too." The kid scoffed, "Mumma. You call her Mumma? Who says that?" I shrugged, bit down on my lip, said nothing, wrapped the snowman in my scarf, and trudged off.

Peer pressure hammered down that day. I felt bad enough that my mother wasn't capable of functioning the way other mothers did, but to know that the name I called her wasn't socially acceptable either, kicked at my insides. I made a mental note to myself right then—do not call her Mumma around anyone but family.

Other than that incident, I got a thrill out of school and the friends I was making. My first kindergarten crush was

Ed. He had curly, blondish, hair and we played on the monkey bars together during recess. During one playtime, while hanging from my knees with my arms dangling underneath me, I plummeted to the ground. 'Revoir,' as he was called, jumped off his perch, helped me to the nearby window seat, and looked after me; such a gentleman at such a tender age.

Happily, upon returning home that afternoon, I shared my exciting news about this boy I met at school. Mumma frowned, "I don't want you playing with boys." I couldn't understand why it made her angry. He was kind, adorable, and he helped me. Not long after, I detailed my adventures about another boy I liked, William. She demanded, "Stay away from the boys, they're trouble." From that conversation forward, I never mentioned to her any boys that I played with or thought were cute. I kept those thoughts to myself. Instead, I redirected my attention to school activities and participated in every club I could.

In fourth grade, I participated in the annual Spring Choral performance with the high school students at Luther L. Wright High School. I was giddy with excitement at this opportunity. I had never stepped foot in such an enormous gymnasium. In between rehearsals, I ran up and down the bleachers from top to bottom. On the day of the show, I was ecstatic. I wore my favorite pale-green, pleated, loosely fitting dress. The day was electric. It was a full house—people clapping for us, and taking pictures. I was elated to be singing with the big kids and was enamored with how our voices permeated the gymnasium. Every single thing about the day was perfect; everything except that my mother wasn't there. I never showed my sadness— never talked about it, but deep inside, I hated that my mother was not able to join in my classroom events. But I dared not express that feeling anywhere, to anyone, ever. I didn't want to make her feel bad nor make her angry. Instead, that afternoon, I dug deep, stood proud, and sang at the top of my lungs, "It's A Small World After All."

Though Mumma couldn't attend events, she was supportive of my activities, and quite often encouraged them. She allowed me to go to a week-long summer camp. All the girls had a huge crush on one camp instructor who went by the name "Bubbles," because of his curly blonde hair. On the last day of the camp, we had a farewell dance, and I got an opportunity to slow dance with him; every girl lined up to dance with him. Of course, I never told Mumma about this daring escapade.

That evening, we were giddy talking about Bubbles. As we were getting ready for bed, I learned the words to the song, "Billy Don't Be a Hero." While undressing, someone asked me why I still wore a T-shirt and not a bra. The question caught me off guard and I felt a pang of self-consciousness grip at my insides. One girl asserted, "I don't wear a bra, either." Well into the wee morning hours, the four of us talked about Bubbles, boys, breasts, and bras. I didn't dare share that I saw my mother's breasts during many a bath.

My mother never wore a bra. During her baths, I washed her chest and underarms. When I initially started bathing her, I was intrigued by her breasts. The skin was wrinkly, and it lay against her bony chest. I was curious why her nipples were so dark. Mine weren't dark. As I ran the washcloth over her nipples she squirmed, frowned, and told me to wash around them. From that bathing episode forward, I learned to discreetly peek at her breasts. After that summer camp excursion, I wondered when I would start wearing a bra.

When I returned home from camp, I quietly entered the bedroom when no one was around, shut the door, and propped a chair in front of it. I shuffled through my sister Debbie's clothes drawer and retrieved her white bra. I held it up and was amazed at how large it was. After struggling to connect the hooks, I figured out it was much too big for my chest. I grabbed a handful of my socks and stuffed the cups. I paraded around the room, marveling at my ample chest.

Later that evening, I waited and waited for my siblings to leave the living room. I got up the courage and sat next to Mumma on the couch and whispered, "Mumma can I start wearing a bra?" "What?" she said. I leaned in closer, "Can I wear a bra?" She raised an eyebrow, "You're not ready to wear a bra." Dejected, I wandered into the kitchen, poured a tall glass of milk, grabbed the brown tin can of Hershey's Syrup from the cupboard, and mindlessly squirted the liquid cocoa into the glass of milk. As I pondered the fate of my adolescent, growing chest, I followed my delightful chocolate drink with a handful of Oreo cookies.

I participated in Brownies, Girl Scouts, and baton classes.

From the confines of her green couch, Mumma taught me and my sister Madeline how to bake cakes for the annual Halloween Festival Cake Walk. Mumma kept all her recipes (from her earlier years) on small, white recipe cards. She instructed Madeline, who methodically followed the written directions. I helped Madeline break the eggs and insisted on licking the cake batter after she whipped up the ingredients.

One time, I got injured playing dodgeball, and Mumma called the principal and admonished him for allowing children to participate in such a horrid sport. As much as I enjoyed Central School, that was about to change.

We were members of St. Ambrose Catholic Church and Mumma managed to send us off to church almost every Sunday. Father Ruppe, the Pastor of the parish, often came to the house to give Mumma communion. We enjoyed his visits and were pleasantly surprised when, in 1971 Father Ruppe arrived at our door and introduced us to Father Sheedlo, the newly appointed assistant priest, who would now take over as the visiting priest. Father Sheedlo was much younger and a much cuter priest than Father Ruppe. Madeline was smitten. I admit his wavy black hair and his beaming smile behind that beard were charming, but Madeline absolutely adored him.

Her crush on Father Sheedlo didn't go unnoticed by any of us. We teased her relentlessly every time we saw his car pull up to the house. He was considerate, welcoming, and had a sense of humor that made us feel at ease. After he left, Madeline swooned, and like clockwork, she trotted off to the bedroom, put on her "Sound of Music" album, and sang along with every song for hours, likely imagining herself as one of the nuns.

These priest visits were fine with me until he actually convinced my mother that we should go to Catholic school. I was utterly against it. Central School was my treasured getaway and I cherished my friends. Mumma stated she could not afford the tuition, but Father Ruppe assured her that our education costs would be nominal. Mumma caved. I was beside myself. Madeline, of course, who had yearned to be a nun as long as I could remember, was bubbling over with excitement at this proposal.

It was fifth grade when I was sent off to Ironwood Catholic Grade School. The principal, Sister Dorothy Ann, was kind to me and helped me feel less anxious. I thrived in spelling bee contests and eagerly awaited gym class activities which were held in the cafeteria. We moved the tables and chairs aside, and either climbed ropes, did jumping jacks, or learned how to square dance. Everything about this religious institution was fine—until one day I was talking with a classmate during class and Sister John Marie punished me (not the other kid) by making me spend the rest of class in the supply closet. Embarrassed, I scampered to the three-foot-by-three-foot punishment dungeon, and she shut the door. Darkness enveloped me. I nestled up to the shelf of supplies, sat on the ice-cold, cement floor, and bawled my eyes out for the rest of that class. I never talked in her class again.

Like most children, I adapted. It helped that there was a

balance of laypeople and parochial staff. Sister Priscilla was quite stern, yet passionate about ensuring her students grasped the importance of the English language. So passionate was she to instill in us the importance of properly spoken English, she created the "No And, Um, and But Club." Each week we trudged up to the front of the class and spoke about a topic near and dear to us. We were keenly aware of the prying eyes and sensitive ears of Sister Priscilla in the back of the room taking tally for every uttered 'Um,' 'But,' and 'And.'

During one geography assignment, Mr. Krznarich provided a fun opportunity to create our own urban cities. I spent hours on this school project ensuring that my imaginary city had trees on every block, a post office, a grocery store, laundromat, skating rink, a magnificent, lush park with a multitude of swing sets, candy stores, a theater, and a hospital. Sister Marie Williams, a fun and feisty character, made science class an adventure. I proudly constructed my own radio from scratch and a fully functioning, erupting volcano for the annual science fair.

Music class with Sister James Ellen was my favorite. She was a gentle lady with a bright, infectious smile who proudly shared stories about Hawaii. During one choir practice, she encouraged me to take private and group guitar lessons. We couldn't afford a guitar, so my easygoing brother Ricky, who was eleven years older, gave me his electric guitar. It wasn't easy for me to play, especially the way he did, since he was super strong and considerably taller than I was. The electric guitar was an obstacle, but

Sister James Ellen assured me we'd find a solution, and waived the lesson fee. The guitar captivated me. As with everything I did, I threw myself wholeheartedly into learning to play the instrument. I spent hours at Johnson's Music store obsessing over all the music books and finger charts.

During private lessons I was fine because the room was quiet and my guitar could be heard. But when we had group lessons, I was continually embarrassed since everyone had an acoustic guitar, and Sister James Ellen had me compensate for the electric guitar because of the metal strings and the pressure I had to use. And, of course, I didn't have a speaker to plug the guitar into, so it was awkward for everyone to accommodate the girl with the muffled, very quiet electric guitar. On occasion, I glanced up and caught a glimpse of kids snickering or rolling their eyes. I was ecstatic when I finally had saved enough allowance money and income from my newspaper route to get an acoustic guitar—I finally fit in with the rest of my fellow guitar players.

In addition to guitar lessons and performances, I immersed myself in various school activities. It got me out of the house and allowed me to spend time with my friends. Choir, theater, cheerleading, and forensics were among my favorites. As long as I did well in school—which I did—Mumma encouraged my extracurricular activities with friends.

I cherished my school friends. Not only were they fun to be around, but I felt safe with them. In my younger years, I was overly excited every time I got to play at Susan Bishop's house. It was a massive, brown house. I felt I could get lost in it for days when we played hide-and-seek. Andy Kuula, Anita Simmons, Fran Balduc, Wanda, and Jean were among my closest friends. I got a thrill out of visiting their houses, too. My friends' parents were kind and welcomed me with open arms. It was odd, yet comforting, to observe mothers who greeted us at the door or cooked a meal. I marveled at this. They consistently made me feel special. There were moments I secretly wished that their mother could be my mother.

They ensured we had food or treats before we went outside to play. They frequently invited me to dinner or a sleepover. Their respective houses were huge, compared to ours. My siblings and I often got teased by school kids because we lived in a round, tin-roofed hut. I withstood the taunting and swallowed the shame I inwardly experienced. Yet, my close friends accepted me for who I was. They couldn't care less that we were a low-income family and dwelled in a corrugated tin, half-domed rental with a bed-ridden mother. Now and again they asked how my mother was. I didn't recognize it as pity or curiosity on their part, just friendship.

On the contrary, Mumma wasn't supportive of my having new friends over. It made her uncomfortable. One day I made a new friend on the playground, and after much pleading, Mumma yielded. It was after school, and when Karen and I entered our little hut, I introduced her to my mother. Karen was polite but was taken aback by seeing my mother housebound. She went to shake my mother's hand, and of course, my mother couldn't offer her hand in exchange. It was an awkward moment. Everyone in school knew that my mother was bedridden. But, to hear 'bedridden' is very different from coming face-to-face with a paralyzed woman lying on her green couch, unable to extend her hand.

I ushered Karen into the bedroom. We pulled out our books to study, but Karen was intrigued, and she peppered me with questions. "Can she walk at all? How does she go to the bathroom? Do you have to feed her?" I shrugged it off and changed the subject. Yet, at that moment I decided to never have a new friend over again.

Artist unknown

Dog Down Under

Sundays had a melancholy feeling about them. One Sunday, a deep-rooted anxiety permeated the air in our house. I will never forget that nightmarish day.

A painting hung in our bedroom that made me both lonely and hopeful. It was of three youthful girls in delicate, loose-fitting, snowy-white dresses with pink ribbons in their hair, and a young boy in dark shorts who grasped his taller sister's hand while they danced around a towering tree. In the background was a stately, white, Victorian mansion.

I often gazed at that painting and daydreamed. I longed for the children on the canvas to be me, my sisters, and my brother. Their lives appeared fanciful and free of any worldly responsibility—a sharp contrast to our accommodations and childhood of weighty responsibilities.

As beautiful as it was, the image made me sad. The mansion was distant, the uncut grass was dry and brownish-yellow, the boy was desperately clutching his sister's hand with both of his, as if trying to hold on, and the tree was barren. Perhaps every family does experience some sadness.

Yet, I grasped onto the dream of a happy and safe family life.

I sometimes wondered why my other siblings lived with my dad and only Kelly and I lived with our mother. I was thrilled when Debbie moved to Ironwood. Madeline moved soon after—both moves at the court's request. While we waited for the legal processing, Madeline and I spent many a night talking on the phone. I sprawled out on the large green chair, phone in hand, gazing out of the window at the stars, and sang "Twinkle, Twinkle Little Star." Though miles apart, we bonded over telephone conversations and melodies, both of us overjoyed about living together. However, something changed once she moved in with us.

Mumma had devised ways to maintain her rules within the walls of our two-bedroom, weather-beaten hut. She inherently used our unique insecurities and weaknesses to manage what she, in her bedridden state, could not otherwise accomplish. In particular, Mumma had a stronghold on Madeline, the middle sister. Unlike with Debbie and me, she mentally controlled Madeline. Debbie was the oldest and argued with Mumma. I was the youngest and completely surrendered and hid in fear. Madeline was stuck in the middle, and it was she who carried out my mother's ruthless demands.

Prior to moving to Ironwood, Madeline underwent testing and didn't measure up to the state standard; so when she started Central School, she was sent to a 'special education' class. Madeline became withdrawn and resorted to music as a way to cope within a dysfunctional family unit. She was obsessed with the "Sound of Music" and disappeared into the bedroom and sang along with the album for hours. She had a beautiful soprano voice and performed in local events throughout her school years. For the most part, however, her childhood was fraught with desolation and disappointment.

It was the 1970s, and there was little compassion for anyone outside the norm. Throughout her grade school years, she had to withstand taunting because of her placement in Special Ed. Each morning when we trotted off to our regular classrooms, I observed Madeline shuffle down the short hallway toward the 'special' classroom. Unfortunately, school was not the only place Madeline endured ridicule. Mumma often criticized her for her intellectual shortcomings. On more than one occasion, she'd browbeat Madeline, calling her 'dumb.' That was only one of a multitude of ways Mumma controlled Madeline. She had a tormented childhood. Time and time again, I felt sorry for her.

Although Madeline could be affectionate and caring, she could also be insensitive. I suspect she inherited her callousness and cold streak from Mumma. Madeline was well aware that Mumma's silent treatment was an effective punishment for me, so she used the same neglect-and-ignore tactic. I was sitting on the rollaway bed that only years earlier was our dancing pad. This incident was different. I was eating a piece of her Brach's candy when she entered. She scowled, "Is that mine?" I couldn't lie. I nodded while chomping on the raspberry-flavored caramel candy. She marched over to the closet where she had hidden her stash. She pulled the bag out from the deep recesses of the shelf, held up the half-empty bag, sauntered over to me, then poked me with her finger. "Give them back." "I only took one," I lied. She knew better and pushed me onto the bed. I emptied my pockets. "I knew it. You stole. I'm telling Mumma."

"No. Don't. I'm sorry. I won't take them again." She scoffed, and stared me down. My apology wasn't sufficient.

Then it came. Like clockwork. She folded her arms and smirked.

I knew that smirk—it was the one Madeline made immediately before ignoring me for as long as humanly possible. Without fail, it worked. She and Mumma knew my weakness. Ignore me and I will buckle and fold like my Raggedy Ann doll.

And so, for the entire rest of the day, she shunned me. No matter how much I begged for her to talk to me she continued to ignore me. Throughout the day I pleaded with her. By bedtime, I guess she tired of my groveling. We crawled into bed, "Madeline, please. Say something. Whatever I did. I'm sorry." She pulled the blankets up over her and snickered, "I guess."

I turned over onto my side and was left there wondering why my sister hated me so much. This power play between us lingered throughout our childhood. Inevitably, each and every time, regardless of what went wrong or who was at fault, I begged and pleaded for forgiveness. She forced me to admit she was the top dog every chance she could.

Yet, as uncompassionate and cold as she could be, my sister also had a nurturing side. She didn't have a choice. Mumma insisted she watch over me. Once, I had a terrible flu, and Madeline checked in on me and sat next to me on the bed. I was burning up, and she gently rested her hand on my forehead. As she tenderly stroked my forehead, I was comforted by her soothing touch. She momentarily left the room and returned with a bowl of Campbell's Chicken Noodle soup and sat beside me while I ate. Calmed by her presence, I fell asleep with my dog Peppy snuggled beside me.

🐾 🐾 🐾

We had two dogs while I was growing up—Peppy and Princess. Peppy was a friendly, medium-large, brownish-yellow dog with white paws and underside who freely wandered the neighborhood, and kept himself entertained by chasing cars. Many a time I witnessed Peppy barking at the rotating wheels of the occasional car as it drove up our street.

On summer weekends, we played doggie dress-up and adorned him with our undershirts, underwear, and socks. After withstanding our wardrobe play, Peppy wandered off and returned later in the evening with the clothes tattered and torn. Our canine companion also kept Mumma company while we were at school and was the well-loved family dog for a great deal of my childhood.

At some point, Ricky gave us his dog, Princess. Mumma wasn't fond of having another dog, but he assured Mumma that if it didn't work out, he would take her back home with him. Ricky was one of her favorite children and Mumma would do anything for him; so Princess found herself in a new home. She was a quiet, medium-large, cream-colored dog. We were used to Peppy wandering off for hours at a time, but it was different with Princess. Mumma perpetually cautioned us—"Do not let her roam the neighborhood," she'd yell, "especially when she's in heat." We didn't listen. We let Princess out of the house— free as a bird. As kids we didn't understand and just thought Mumma was being strict. It wasn't fair that Peppy got to tramp around the neighborhood, so why couldn't Princess? We would soon learn a chilling lesson once Princess became pregnant.

As children we were fascinated at the prospect of puppies, but Mumma had warned us time and again that we could not keep the dogs. The Sunday evening Princess gave birth, the energy in the house was high. We were mesmerized as Princess pushed each rat-like creature from her canine womb. Then, seemingly out of nowhere, the excitement turned to horror. Mumma yelled from the other room, "Get rid of them."

Madeline and I glanced at each other in shock. No way! But Mumma was relentless.

"But how?" Madeline shrieked.

Mumma shouted, "Flush them down the toilet."

Madeline sobbed, "No, Mumma, no!"

"Do it. Now!" Mumma barked.

Madeline gingerly picked up a harmless, innocent, wee mutt.

"Go!"

Madeline held the canine close. She was in hysterics— and then shut down her emotions and robotically listened as Mumma insisted she kill the puppies.

That evening I learned the harsh reality that a mother doesn't need to be mobile to psychically control her children. Madeline succumbed to Mumma's demands.

Madeline headed toward the bathroom. As Mumma yelled from the other room to "flush them," I pleaded with

Madeline not to kill them. But, it was as if she was possessed. I tore at her shirt, but she pushed me aside and
marched blindly to the soon-to-be doggie deathtrap.

I observed in horror as the slimy newborn pup wiggled in
her hands, its eyes tightly shut. Then Madeline buckled and
knelt down in front of the toilet.

Mumma was yelling, Madeline was shaking, and I was
crying. It was as if an explosion of anger, confusion, and
panic swirled around all of us—connected us in a tsunami
of death. Madeline dangled the defenseless puppy dog over
the toilet bowl.

I plopped down on the floor next to the porcelain death
trap as the pup's feet squirmed over the ice-cold water. I
grabbed Madeline's wrist one last time. She shoved me
aside. She squeezed hard on its tiny neck. Suspended over
the toilet bowl, it seemed an eternity until ultimately, the
life went from its limbs. She yanked hard on the silver
handle. The flushing water, the lifeless pup swirling into the
abyss—it was too much for my brain and my heart.

By the third canine euthanasia, I was numb. I don't recall
how many puppies Madeline flushed down the toilet, but it
was too many. I fled from the bathroom into the bedroom.
I grabbed my doll Marella and held her tight and buried
my head under the pillow. But nothing could dampen
Mumma's barking of orders as Madeline carried out the
barbaric drownings. I cried myself to sleep. How could
Madeline do this? How could Mumma do this? How could
anyone do this? No one talked of this incident again; Ricky
had no idea what had happened to Princess's pups, and
she never gave birth again.

Regardless of this atrocious event, for some reason some of the pups were allowed to live. I do not remember why, but what I do remember is one afternoon I was alone in one of the two bedrooms. My siblings were outside playing, and I was sitting on the floor with the pups between my legs. They were scurrying around when suddenly something washed over me, and in a flash, I snatched a puppy and I shoved it across the dark, wooden, splintered floor— its blonde-and-caramel-speckled body flailed as it bounced up against the light-green wall. In the same instant, I thought—this puppy doesn't deserve that. I hoisted the precious pooch into my arms and caressed it against my chest while tears ran down my cheeks. I didn't know what prompted such behavior. How could I do this? The pups eventually found a new home. I concealed this unspeakable act, and I promised myself I would never do that again. I lived by that promise.

My brother Greg cradles our dog, Princess. Wendy holds her
nephew Brandon, Kelly nestled between us. Winter 1976.

Dark Dreams

There is a Native American sentiment, something to the effect that our dream life is an indicator of our daytime physical realities. Nighttime dreams give us the opportunity to explore situations at a deeper level than when we are in our daytime, waking state. As an adult, I came to understand that my childhood night terrors were indicative of what was truly going on emotionally for me in relationship to my mother and family. During the waking hours, I could pretend and fantasize a wanderlust-filled life, and shut out any despair or fear I was experiencing. But my dreams didn't lie.

For a predominant part of my childhood I lived in fear—fear of my mother dying, fear of being taken away from our mother by Social Services, fear of the harsh reality of a pain-riddled and volatile mother. Huddled inside our dwelling in the evening hours, I found my place on the floor and imagined far distant worlds while constructing and dressing my paper dolls, drawing fragmented, mechanical sketches on my Etch-A-Sketch, or playing a familiar game of solitaire or a game of Jacks. When bored, I played a card game of Slap Jack or Pick-up Sticks with my siblings. In the frosty winter evenings, board games of Life or Monopoly kept us entertained.

Most of the time, however, television was our refuge. It was the family's way to cope. The Tom Jones variety show was Mumma's favorite. We watched his weekly show religiously and it didn't take long for him to become my first celebrity crush. Carol Burnett and Hee Haw variety shows lightened the mood. If you craved spine-tingling thrills, you watched Frankenstein, The Wolfman, Night-stalker, or Night Gallery while huddled close to Mumma on the couch or on the floor nearby. Unfortunately, these scary, haunted, television exploits only magnified the nightmares I encountered as a child.

They were dark. The surreal nightmares brought forth evil creatures lurking in the room next door. I heard them first, rustling in the closet in that room. Their chatter grew louder as the hellish creatures shuffled down the hallway. They edged along the walls and peered around my bedroom door with eerie, white-glazed eyes. Inching closer to the bottom of the bed, the stunted creatures tore at my feet then snatched me off the bed into utter darkness. The movie villain Freddy Kreuger was angelic compared to these hellish, ghastly creatures who tormented me nearly every night. I did everything in my power to stave them off in the witching hours. But it was futile.

A painting of a lone, silver tree encased in a glass picture frame hung on the bedroom wall. Its shiny, gnarled branches stretched across the sky-blue canvas background. I tortured myself to keep awake as I stared, studying each and every twisted silver limb for hours in the darkness while listening to Mumma's breathing as I lay beside her.

Before she moved to the green couch in the living room, Mumma took refuge in the bedroom. Often, she preferred that I sleep with her. How could I tell her 'no'? How could

I confide that my grim, horrific terrors also included my mother, who morphed into a wicked witch? In my half-awake dream state, I couldn't turn or move as she thrashed at the center of my back with her bony, prickly fingers. I was panicked, powerless, paralyzed—beyond terrified. The astral travels had a menacing, macabre way of reminding me how oppressed and fearful I truly was. As intensely as I tried, I could not escape the dark dreams.

Once, I talked in my sleep and apparently disclosed some unhappy feelings about my mother. The following morning, she scolded me harshly and screamed that I didn't love her. I pleaded with her to believe me that I did love her, but she refused to listen. She declared that my sleep-talking was how I truly felt about her. How could I defend my dreams? I was at a loss.

She brought this sleep-talking episode up time and time again. If I misbehaved, she reminded me that I didn't love her. I begged for forgiveness. She scoffed then ignored me. This pattern continued for years. I felt as if I had been abandoned by my own mother. I was doubly frightened to fall asleep for fear I'd dream-chatter in my sleep state. During my waking hours, I relentlessly did everything in my power to prove to her that she meant the world to me, in the event I talked in my sleep again.

I was alone in my dream world—defenseless and at the mercy of the shrunken, monstrous, diabolical creatures. Once I shared with my mother that I was having nightmares. She scoffed, "They're just dreams." They weren't just dreams. They were monumental, agonizing occurrences that scarred my psyche. No one could save me or rescue me. I felt isolated and alone and terribly frightened each and every evening when it was time for bed.

But nighttime passed into dawn, and the sun rose again.

Wendy with her grandfather. Here I am with
Gramps at the foot of Hiawatha. A favorite place
where I often played. July 1970.

Swing Set and a Tree

The outdoors was my escape. It was my freedom. In the summer months, as soon as Mumma got her bedpan, her sponge bath, and the chores were finished, we sprinted outside to the lush, green, abundant landscape of Northern Michigan.

Ironwood was a small town located on US Highway 2, located at the westernmost tip of the Upper Peninsula (U.P.). Our house was situated a few blocks from the Wisconsin border in close proximity to the Montreal River. Gogebic County was rich with Native American culture. As a child, I spent many an hour playing at the base of Hiawatha's feet, the "Tallest Indian in the World." I gazed up in awe at the mammoth 52-foot tall statue. I visualized myself nestled in his arm, surveying the land from his vantage point across the vast Lake Superior.

Iron ore mining was popular at the turn of the century in Ironwood. Our one-story, prefabricated structure of corrugated, galvanized steel (aka Quonset hut) was owned by Ashland Mining Company. When the mines dried up, they deeded the property to Bill Champion, who was our landlord. By the time I came along, ore mining was obsolete; but vast 'caves,' as they were known, were left behind. Right across the street from our property was one of these mammoth caves—remnants of a bygone era. In reality, they were massive dugouts of land grown over with trees and brush. My siblings and I explored the caves for hours to challenge ourselves to see how far to the bottom we could travel. Lumbering along, we snacked on berries from the wild bushes, and loaded our pockets with Native American arrowheads or other miniature relics buried under red pockets of iron ore. We trekked back up the ravines, careful to avoid poison ivy. It only took one or two outbreaks to recognize and steer clear of those glossy, three-leaf clusters.

If Mumma insisted we stay close to the house on any certain day, we either jumped rope on the sidewalk bordering the towering, aromatic, purple lilac bush, hunted for four-leaf clovers, played hopscotch, or picked dandelions and made wishes as we blew the fluff off. My wish was always the same—that Mumma could walk again. After sunset, we played hide-and-seek, chased fireflies, or sprawled on the front lawn gazing at the twirling, spiraling, northern lights when they happened to visit the northern hemisphere.

Bats were typical at dusk. They swooped down as we ducked and dodged, escaping their treacherous claws. On one occasion, Madeline was a target of a bat gone wild that (thinking back) probably got tangled in her hair by accident. But as children, we were convinced the bats were out to get us.

They were not the only creatures out to get us.

Most evenings upon returning home, we had 'tick' check. On one particular tick-check evening, I was the host of an eight-legged creature. It secured a home behind my ear. Of course, I was petrified it was sucking all of my blood. After I calmed down, Mumma used her good hand and tried to evict the squiggly, blood-thirsty creature, but was unable. It found a host and wasn't going to give up so easily. Mumma instructed Madeline to burn the tick with a match then twist it out with tweezers. It took forever to dislodge the now plump, blood-filled, diabolical creature. It ultimately met its death in the toilet bowl. From that point forward, when returning home in the evening during the summer months, tick check was a nightly ritual.

I was fascinated by trees, especially trees that I could climb. On a knoll a short distance from our house there was a substantial grove of trees of varying heights. I always had a myriad of trees to scale. One tree was my favorite. It was about 20-to-30 feet tall and had a sizeable starter limb. I couldn't reach it when I was smaller, so one of my siblings lifted me, and I grabbed hold of the branch. In the beginning, I was afraid to climb to the top, so I sat on the starter limb and hung upside down from my knees and swung back and forth. In time, I grew tall enough and brave enough to squirrel my way up and between the limbs. We challenged each other to see who could climb the fastest and the highest. I took pleasure in the quiet moments and often went off by myself and ascended my favorite tree . . . perched like a bird, scanning the horizon, singing at the top of my lungs.

My refuge—my happy place—was swinging. I could spot a swing set a mile away. If I was stressed or discouraged, I hopped on my bike and rode to a neighboring park a few blocks from our house off Buskirk Road. In reality, it was a substantial, unkempt, grass-covered area that had a red swing set and a teeter-totter. I spent hours on the swing, lost in my imagination, oblivious to the world around me. I indulged in a fantasy world of pretending to be anyone but Wendy. This activity satisfied my need to be in control and feel safe. As I swung back and forth, I sang a multitude of songs: "The Day That I was Young" (Roy Clark), "Sunrise, Sunset" (Fiddler on the Roof), "Downtown" (Petula Clark), and "Delilah" (Tom Jones) were some of my favorites. As I sang, I assumed the character of someone other than Wendy—a person who was respected and appreciated. Hours passed in this wanderlust reverie. The sun was lower in the sky. Time to go home. Some days it was difficult to drop the daydream and return to being Wendy.

When my siblings joined me on the swings, however, it was all fun and games. We liked the swing games where we shared a swing, either with one sibling sitting on the shoulders of another sibling, or one sitting on another's lap, with one person facing one way while the other person faced the opposite way. Other times, we didn't want to share the swing, and we'd fight about who could sit down on the seat, while the other person spun them around until the chain was coiled up and then quickly untwirled them. We often dared each other as to who could jump from the swing at the highest point. One time, Madeline swung so high that when she jumped, she crashed and broke her arm. We never played that dare game again.

One day, while walking home from school, I stumbled across the Carnegie Library on Aurora Street. The gray steps leading up to the red-brick fortress beckoned me inward. I encountered a piece of heaven in the quiet solitude.

From that day forward, I often slipped into the sanctuary of books and spent hours tucked in the fantasy section sitting on the cold, tiled floor, imagining a world of giants and beanstalks, damsels searching for their lost silver slipper, or children alone in a sinister forest ruled by wicked witches who wanted to eat them.

I suppose, as in any big family, siblings form cliques, and each child finds his or her own coping mechanisms. For me, it was retreating into an abundant fantasy life with my brother Greg. Until he moved full time from my dad's in Bessemer to Ironwood, Greg visited quite often on the weekends and stayed with us during the summer months. Greg was my best friend and confidant. He had as rich and vivid an imagination as I did, and therefore, we bonded quickly. We understood each other.

During our make-believe playtimes, I insisted we live in California, and Greg's requirement was that he be a girl with blonde hair. I was down with that. I had no idea Greg was gay (in the 60s and 70s there was no way he could have safely come out). As far as I was concerned, we were sisters joined in a fanciful world all our own. I wholeheartedly believed he was a girl for those chosen playtime moments.

There was a broken-down, forest-green car in our yard that belonged to Ricky. It didn't work—just a piece of junk—but it was rich with a world of possibilities for Greg and me. We determined the parameters of our world for that day's play—who were the bad guys chasing us, and what city or state we were in—it was a toss-up between Florida or California.

First and most importantly, we had to discreetly retrieve Madeline's short, yellow, ruffled slip from her dresser drawer. It was a vital prop, as it was Greg's golden-blonde hair. He insisted on having blonde hair, and once the slip was firmly secured with bobby pins, he gleefully tossed his head to and fro. After his hairdressing was in place, the next order of business was what names we would choose. Inevitably, Greg chose the name Veronica, and I decided on Vicki. And so, with a short, yellow slip atop his head and an imagination pulsating with frothy fantasy, Veronica and I took our places behind the steering wheel, and we were off on our road trip across the country, lost for hours in our fabulous, fantastical world.

Other afternoons, the hood of the green car transformed into our pretend Broadway stage. We belted out any one of our favorite tunes, "Somewhere Over the Rainbow," "Hello Dolly," or "Oklahoma," to a throng of thousands. Greg was the best sister a girl could have.

But those whimsical flights only lasted so long. The street lights flickered on, and once again it was time to take off the golden hair, descend from the playland clouds, head back to the house, and return to reality.

Wendy, age two. I still like boiled eggs. May 1965.

The Hand That Feeds You

Mumma had one good, working hand. It was her smoking hand. Though her left hand was slightly paralyzed, she had some use of it, especially in the beginning years. If she had trouble lighting a cigarette, she had us help her. I was fascinated at how she smoked her cigarettes. It was as if she was sucking every bit of life from those slender white sticks.

What I didn't like, however, was while we were at school she poured water on the smokes in her ashtray to ensure the cigarettes were entirely out. Inevitably, once home from a day of studies, one of us was asked to "dump the ashtray." I hated that chore. The ashtray was packed with stale, ashen goop and the stench was stifling. I begrudgingly picked up the aquamarine ashtray and trudged off to the bathroom.

I grabbed a wad of toilet paper and thoroughly wiped out the rancid remains and flushed it down the toilet. When I was older and a bit braver, I had to understand why Mumma liked smoking. So once, when she asked me to dump out the ashtray, there was one cigarette that was still fairly long. I sneaked outside with it, put a match to it, and took a puff. Putrid. How could she possibly enjoy that?

In addition to her obsession with her Pall Mall cigarettes, she savored her Folgers Coffee. Every morning Madeline or Debbie made her a pot of coffee, carried the cup into the living room, and placed it on the TV tray. When it came time to open a fresh can of coffee, I pushed my way into the kitchen and hopped on the kitchen chair, making sure I was the one to open it. I absolutely relished the savory smell of Folgers and the popping sound the tin can created when it opened. I placed the red-and-white can under the electric can opener and fixated on the cover as it rotated under the grooves, then burst to release the hearty, robust aroma. I shoved my face over the top of the can and sucked in the fresh scent of the roasted, ground coffee.

As a result of her impairment, Mumma had difficulty drinking her coffee, or any liquids for that matter. She often asked one of us to give her a drink. She cranked her neck and lifted her head toward the cup. This took practice. Many times in the beginning years, if I didn't position the cup just right, the refreshment ran down her chin and onto her nightgown. The defeated look on her face when this happened, the way her lip quivered, and how she lowered her eyes, left an imprint on my mind that stays with me even now, especially at night when I reach over to get a sip of water while in bed.

Other times, she yelled at me in frustration, grabbed hold of my wrist with her working hand, and steered the cup correctly toward her mouth. As years went on, we determined that having her drink with a straw was the better option.

Grooming of Mumma's entire body was part of our regular routine, except for her teeth. I have no memory of her ever asking us to brush her teeth. To this day, I do not understand why. Every now and again she asked one of us to bring her some Listerine so she could rinse her mouth.

She never went to the dentist, but she never had dental problems, either. She had beautiful teeth as a healthy woman, so perhaps her pearly whites were extra durable in spite of the fact the rest of her body was under attack. She insisted, however, that we went to the dentist, even though our dentist visits were more like torture. I suspect because the state was paying for our dental care, the dentists couldn't be bothered with a shot of Novocaine.

It was a complete failure when I first learned to wash my mother's hair. I retrieved the Prell shampoo from the bathroom, filled a bucket with warm water, and carried it carefully to the couch. I squeezed out the green, herbal liquid and lathered my mother's hair and scalp. At one point, she wanted to rub the shampoo in herself. Her hand was shaky, but she was distributing the sudsy shampoo equally over her scalp. During the rinse cycle, which consisted of pouring copious cups of water to rinse out the shampoo, she actually managed to pour a couple of cups over her head, until, well—I tipped the bucket—water spilling everywhere. Needless to say, it wasn't long after that episode that Mumma decided that the preferable choice for hair grooming was dry shampoo.

We took turns cutting Mumma's nails. Her fingernails were a dull yellow color and hard; but not as hard as her toenails. I dreaded when she asked me to trim her toenails because it was like cutting curled cement. The first time I trimmed her nails, I pinched the skin on one of her toes and drew blood. She shrieked. It pained me, knowing that I hurt her. I preferred giving her a sponge bath, bedpan, or even an enema—it was less stressful.

I studied my mother's hands when I bathed her or lit her cigarette. I was fascinated by the lines and veins that ran across her knuckles. Though divorced, she wore her wedding ring. She often reminded me that when she died, I would get her diamond ring. The sparkling white gem stood in contrast to her weathered, bony hands. She informed me that her hands were wrinkled because she worked hard all her life. I lifted my hand up to hers and examined my smooth knuckles and fingers that were silky by comparison and worried I didn't work as hard as she had. She chuckled and explained that I was too young to have rough hands and assured me that I was an excellent worker.

Sometimes I had to remove the ring because her hands were hurting or swollen. On one of these painful occasions, the ring wouldn't come off. We smothered her finger in Vaseline and then Mazola oil and, after much commotion, the ring finally slipped off. More often than not, she kept the ring on the TV tray where it sat nestled between her ashtray and the pill bottles.

Every so often, Mumma asked me to clean the ring. One time, as she reached for her cup of coffee it spilled all over the TV tray. I grabbed a nearby towel and wiped up the mess. I picked up the coffee-soaked newspaper and the ring underneath. I held up the gemstone, "Want me to wash this off?" Mumma nodded.

While I washed the diamond ring over the sink, I was mindful not to drop it down the drain. I did that once and I was petrified it was lost forever. Thankfully, my brother helped me retrieve it. While I rinsed off the gem under the running water, I gazed at the diamond, catching glints of light. I often wondered why she kept the wedding ring. She never talked fondly of Dad. Regardless, it was a beautiful ring, and it made me feel exceptional, knowing that Mumma entrusted me with this precious gift.

When I was done rinsing off the gemstone, I slipped the ring on my finger. It was too big. I fussed with the ring for a moment and glanced over at the kitchen table where Madeline was doing her homework. She glared at me, "She favors you more, that's why you're getting it."

"No, she doesn't," I sighed. We'd had this conversation before.

"Yeah, she does. You know it." She went back to her homework.

I shrugged, removed the ring, and left the kitchen.

It wasn't my fault that my mother favored some of us more than others.

Wendy and Kelly, mid-1970s.

A Screen Door Away
from Freedom

Winters were harsh in the U.P. Even the locals complained about the biting, freezing winds and temperatures so far below zero, exposed human flesh would freeze if one stayed outside for more than a few minutes. Hundreds of inches of snow fell every year. Winter in "Big Snow Country" was to be endured, survived, and occasionally enjoyed by those rugged enough to brave the elements for sledding, snowball fights, ice skating at the Colonial Ice Skating Rink, or skiing at any of the exciting, downhill ski resorts.

We often woke to snowdrifts under our front door, even after stuffing a towel in the cracks—which acted as our form of weather-stripping—where cold air's icy fingers shoved through.

Once, there was a mega snow storm. It dumped heaps of snow across the Great Lakes region; so much snow, in fact, we couldn't get out of the house. Unable to open our front door, we were trapped for a couple of days. One can only play so many games of solitaire, fashion clothing lines for your paper dolls, or create masterpiece cakes in the Easy Bake Oven. At some point, the feelings of loneliness and claustrophobia set in. The blistering, frigid weather was nothing compared to the harsh reality that my mother could be, at any moment, intensely cruel. She ruled us with an ironclad, psychological fist.

I had seven brothers. Of them, Kelly and Johnny had the most impact on me for two different reasons.

Johnny was the third oldest. As a toddler, he contracted pneumonia, which ultimately led to his mental retardation (as it was known in the 1970s). Shortly after the divorce of my parents and at the request of the Gogebic County's Social Services, he was institutionalized for mental retardation at Newberry State Hospital when he was around ten years old. Johnny lived at the hospital for a number of years and, for some reason, which I do not remember, he was allowed to return home. I was ecstatic. Mumma said I could go along with our relative to pick Johnny up at the hospital.

We journeyed the 250-mile passage westward across the vast regions of the U.P. Upon arriving, I exited the car and stood in awe at the colossal and menacing brick building that seemed to stretch for miles across the landscape. Once inside, awe turned to trepidation. There were a lot of stairs. Wide, unending hallways with row after row of closed doors with very small windows near the top, like peepholes; the musty smell of the building and the sun shimmering through the scattering of mesh-wired windows made an impression on me. Although it was a sunlit day, everything about the place was gloomy. I was thrilled to know my brother was coming home to live with us.

Once things settled upon Johnny's return to the family unit, he attended the newly built "Gogebic Area Rehabilitation Council" (GARC). It was a day school for retarded or mentally handicapped adults in Wakefield, a few towns over. Per the Ironwood Daily Globe newspaper, the GARC was designed with the hopes that "despite their handicaps, these people could become productive individuals capable of contributing to society." Johnny was delighted to attend. Each morning a bus arrived and Johnny shuffled across the lawn and boarded the bus. He returned home in the afternoon and proudly shared his activities. On one occasion, Johnny made the local newspaper. There was an article showcasing the GARC, and a photo of Johnny working a loom splashed across the page. Johnny was especially proud, as were we all, including Mumma, who cut out the article and placed it in the photo album.

Johnny was seven years older than me. He had short, disheveled hair and deep-set, dark-brown eyes. He wore a special shoe with a silver brace on his left leg, and as a result, he walked with a limp. One arm was slightly paralyzed, and it was generally tucked close to his side. Regardless of his disability, Johnny was a sinewy powerhouse. He was ruggedly built and prone to temper. One time, he was angry at me because I ate the last scoop of mashed potatoes and he punched me in the arm. I braved the potent force and was left with a bruise to match. Regardless of his mood swings, he and I generally got along.

Even though our residence was snug, we had a large front lawn and the neighbors lived quite a distance from us. In the summer months, Johnny enjoyed mowing the lawn. He tinkered with the lawn mower and didn't appreciate anyone else who touched the machine. He regularly sat on the front steps and waited for the occasional truck to drive by. He limped quickly across the lawn, pumping his functioning arm as if honking to the truck. The truckers tooted their horn in return. It was a highlight of Johnny's day and it warmed my heart when the truckers took the time to return the honk. He was fascinated with tools, cars, the CB radio, and the cassette recorder. He nestled in the bedroom for hours recording his voice and playing it back. Sometimes he wandered off and could be found at either Jupiter's, McLellan's, or Wolverine's Discount stores.

Because of Johnny's disability we often worried when he wandered off. He was prone to epileptic seizures and we were informed that each time he had a seizure a part of his brain would burn away. As a child, I was unaware of the technical terms of his condition. The idea of his brain "burning away" frightened me. One hot summer afternoon, he had a seizure on the front lawn. His entire body pounded and thrusted on the ground. The sweat pouring off his body frightened me. I had never seen someone sweat so profusely. Was it the hot afternoon sun or was it because he was burning up from the inside out? My brother and I each grabbed a leg while Madeline restrained his head. It was difficult because, despite his disabled body, he was brawny, and it took all our strength to control his convulsing body. We were instructed to put a stick or a rigid object in his mouth so he wouldn't bite down on his tongue. We were forever on alert with Johnny.

My other brother, the youngest of the ten children, Kelly, was a slightly built, soft-spoken boy with dark-brown hair and a cherub face. His bright brown eyes and delicate smile masked a childhood gloom that only he and those who lived on McLeod Street were privy to. He was withdrawn and kept to himself. I think this was because Mumma demanded he stay inside while the rest of us played outside. I never really understood why she wouldn't let him play with us. We always asked, and the answer was almost always 'no.' On the rare occasions he could come out to play, I was delighted.

When I was about nine, my siblings and I were playing marbles outdoors at the corner of the house. As usual, Kelly, although he was eight, was not allowed to play. One marble was missing and I was convinced that Kelly stole it. I ran inside. Kelly was sitting on the green recliner with his legs crossed with a lightweight blanket covering him. Mumma was sleeping in the bedroom. I quietly asked him where the marble was. He swore he didn't take it, but I didn't buy it. I lifted up the blanket, and to my surprise, he wasn't wearing any underwear; he was naked from the waist down. We both were startled. Embarrassed, I scurried off. I had never seen a penis before, and I briefly wondered why Kelly didn't have his underwear on—but I had a marble game I had to get back to, so I just let it go.

While the daytime summer months were fun because we could disappear outside for hours, evenings could be unpredictable. It all depended on Mumma's pain level and mood. I learned to detect the evenings of wickedness. The tension bubbled deep within my body. A rising sense of dread washed over me, like an apocalyptic, ominous storm cloud hovering over our humble abode. My body trembled. A cyclone of suffering was about to explode.

Something between Mumma and Kelly was toxic. I don't know why or where this destructive behavior started. It was obvious that she "loved" him differently. I suppose she had tender moments with him, but for the most part, what I remember is that my youngest brother endured an atrociously grim childhood. For some reason, Kelly was the scapegoat upon which Mumma unleashed her fury. It was as if he got under her skin and she was not capable or willing to control her rage. It usually started with a random, scathing comment. She would blame him for something, even the tiniest thing. Guilty or not, he became the target.

The deep underbelly of her anger bubbled up from the abyss. "You're a rat!" she screeched. Her face twisted and contorted as she continued to verbally jab at her son. As her disdain increased and her voice grew louder, I shut down, both physically and emotionally. Her insults were atrocious. She snarled, "You're the devil. You're the one who did this to me. You'll never live to be eighteen. I wish you were never born."

During these hellacious incidents, her vicious taunts and name calling spiraled. The verbal bashings thundered through the walls of the house. The assaults grew tremendously forceful and earsplitting. As she unrelentingly, orally whiplashed him, the energy accumulated like steam in a teapot beyond its boiling point about to explode until ultimately, the words spewed out of her mouth like a dragon's poison tongue—

"GET THE PANCAKE TURNER!"

We ALL knew what horrific catastrophe was about to unfold. It was pandemonium. Johnny or Madeline scrambled into the kitchen, whipped open the cabinet drawer, and produced the wooden-handled, metal torture device.

Mumma hollered, "Beat him, beat him!" If Debbie was ordered to carry out the bashing, she only pretended to hit Kelly and told him to scream, and instead she pounded the bed with the pancake turner.

With Johnny and Madeline, it was different. I think they were possessed and actually enjoyed it. Only once, I witnessed the physical assault in its entirety. I huddled near the oil-burning stove and stood by helplessly as Kelly was dragged into the bedroom. Johnny tossed Kelly atop the bed like a bag of trash, pounced on his frail body, and pinned him down with his legs while Madeline restrained Kelly's shoulders.

As Kelly desperately heaved to free himself, Johnny ferociously beat him, first with his fist, and then with the pancake turner. I couldn't see Kelly's face under this barbaric act. He was smothered and ensnared like a defenseless animal caught in an ungodly, inhumane trap. Madeline's and Johnny's faces looked familiar but surreal, like the creatures in my dreams—unnatural, deformed, twisted, savage. Never again did I watch the walloping for the duration.

The beatings were endured up until my mother passed away. It was always the same. One held him down while the other pummeled him. As I bolted from the room, I caught glimpses of Kelly thrashing on the bed. It was heartbreaking to witness my brother try to free himself from their evil grip. As Kelly's primal screams scorched the air, I fled into the kitchen and found refuge between the fridge and wall. I crouched on my knees and covered my ears. Eventually, his piercing cries subsided. I pictured my brother crouching in the closet, holding his bruised and battered body. Those bloodcurdling screams haunt me to this day.

On other depraved occasions, Mumma's brutal punishments included a white bar of soap. Ultimately, Madeline carried out the infliction. It was an overcast, humid afternoon. I was in the kitchen doing dishes. Mumma was shouting at Kelly. By now, I learned to shut out Mumma's wicked screams. I went somewhere in my head where it was quiet, peaceful, safe. Before I knew it, Madeline charged into the kitchen. She had Kelly by his shirt collar and pushed me aside. She grabbed the bar of soap and shoved it violently into his mouth until he gagged. I stood there petrified, fixated on the ridges on top of the kitchen sink near the faucet. I finally emerged from this trance, and turned to gaze at my brother's ailing face.

Contorted, Kelly's body shook as she pinned him up against the kitchen counter. He gagged. She twisted the three-inch, sinuous, waxen chunk as far back as she could until he swallowed a portion. I grabbed Madeline's arm. Kelly shot backwards and dashed from the room and sheltered himself on the floor between the beds. Sweating, Madeline pushed me aside, threw the cake of soap into the sink and plopped on the tattered, yellow kitchen chair. As if on automatic pilot, I picked up the remaining chunk of soap and carefully positioned it in its proper home atop the kitchen sink, and then bolted outside to my favorite tree and climbed as fast and as high as I could. I spent the rest of the day nestled safely in the limbs of her branches, imagining a fantastical world far beyond the one on McLeod Street.

Mumma sent all us kids to bed hungry some nights as punishment. But with Kelly, it was different—it was sadistic. All too frequently, Mumma intentionally starved him while the rest of us were allowed to eat. I did my best to sneak food to him. We had a black-and-white bear cookie jar that we kept atop the cupboard or fridge. During these starving episodes, Kelly snuck out in the middle of the night and ate some of those cookies. The following morning, she had us check the cookie jar, then accused him of stealing. "You're a rat!" she'd screech. He swore he didn't steal any cookies, but even if Kelly did, it didn't matter—he was hungry. Many days, the dogs ate better than Kelly.

In the summer months, we usually kept the dog bowls outside near the sapling pine trees in the front yard. I opened the screen door one scorching summer afternoon, and as I glanced to my left, I was in utter shock—Kelly was perched over the dog bowls eating their leftover, fly-covered, canned food. That image seared my psyche—Kelly on his knees, hiding under the pine trees, cowering as he found nourishment. Though we were all deprived of emotional sustenance and food, Kelly lived the bleakest childhood existence.

When I had chickenpox, Mumma wouldn't let me go outside. I begged. I pleaded. But it was no use. I was stuck inside to ride out the red itchy bumps. I stood as close to the screen door as possible with my face pressed close up to the rusted, wiry mesh. I absorbed the lush, abundant grass of our front lawn, the mountainous, cumulus clouds floating in the bright Midwestern, summer sky. I couldn't understand—why couldn't I go outside, if only to sit on the splintered, wooden, broken front steps. Instead, I surrendered to my fate. Dreaming. Believing. Wondering. All that was between me and freedom was the screen door. Did my brother Kelly feel that way?

Debbie and Kelly share a special brother-and-sister moment.
One of the rare times Kelly was allowed to play outside.
August 1969.

Tender moment between my mother and me. Shirley sporting her stylish pink curlers as she kneels next to Wendy. October 1964.

Nuggets of Tenderness

In spite of my mother's nefarious moments, I loved her. As callous as she could be, she was also helpless. She needed us. There were nuggets of kindness that eased the heartache of childhood's anguished moments.

I grew anxious each evening when we had to come inside the house from a fun day of play. I couldn't predict what the nighttime hours would foist on us. Would it be oppressive, or would it be relaxing? Some evenings were weighted with melancholy and chaos while other evenings were cheerful and calm. Though a deep underbelly of agony was commonplace in our household, moments of pleasure were sprinkled throughout. I savored those affectionate moments; like a banana turning bad, there were bits I cut off, salvaged, and treasured.

I have only one memory of my mother laughing.

One late autumn evening, Mumma, my brother Greg, and I were watching a comedy movie on TV starring the Bowery Boys. Greg and I were perched as usual on the floor right beneath the TV. There was a scene in the movie that affected us all in the same way. Mumma chuckled and then broke out into laughter. Greg and I glanced at each other—shock!—she never, ever laughed like this. We were so moved by her infectious cackle that we giggled. The amusement was contagious. Greg and I exploded into an uproar of snorting and delirious rapture. I rolled and tossed on the floor and laughed until I peed my pants. I didn't care, the surge of euphoria overrode all self-consciousness. But this hilarious evening was, indeed, the exception.

The norm—Mumma was always in pain of one level or another. The pain was typically located in her feet. Quite often she bellowed, "They're burning up!" Or, she screeched that her feet were stinging cold or felt like they were jack-hammered with a drill, or pricked with a thousand needles. Time and again, I stood by helplessly, powerless to do anything to ease her pain. Her eyes red from crying, she'd scream, "Get the Bengay!" I, or one of my siblings, rubbed her feet or some part of her body with the smelly, sticky, white substance. We should have had stock in Bengay, considering the substantial amount of the product we used throughout her lifetime.

The intense Midwest thunderstorms brought out Mumma's kinder and more intimate side. She either had one of us cuddle beside her, or she encouraged us to play our games. But first, we had to "turn everything off." She instructed us to unplug the TV, the coffeemaker, the lamps, the toaster. We groaned and moaned, "But how can we play cards in the dark?" "Get the candles," she reminded us each time. We persisted and begged to keep one light on, but inevitably, she conveyed the story about when she was on the phone during a storm and the phone got hit with lightning. "I was thrown across the room and lucky to be alive," she reminded us. We never won the argument and shuffled off to gather the emergency supply of candles.

During the crackle and pop of lightning and thunder, we played checkers or our favorite board games of Life and

Monopoly. If board games got boring, we played card games like Go Fish, or the seemingly never-ending card game of War. One time, during a thunderstorm, we played Twister, and I peeked over at Mumma propped up and supported by her plethora of pillows. Her face shimmered in the candlelight as she smiled while observing us maneuver the rows of colored dots on the white plastic mat. Once we were sent to bed, I huddled up next to the wall as the thunder boomed and lightning tore across the sky. When I was much younger, the lightning frightened me. Madeline comforted me and said that when it rained, angels were mopping the floors in heaven. When the boom of thunder bellowed overhead, an angel dropped the bucket. I believed that story for many a moon.

I was always curious why Mumma had MS. How did she get it? Where did it start? Answers to the malady of MS in those days were scarce. She didn't like to talk about the disease very much, but every now and again she would talk about her MS, especially when the annual Jerry Lewis Muscular Dystrophy (MD) Telethon was on TV during Labor Day weekend. While Jerry Lewis paraded his entourage of guests throughout the 22-hour broadcast, I asked Mumma, "What's the difference between MS and MD?" She couldn't answer. She really didn't know.

"How'd you get it, Mumma?"

She shrugged, "Don't know. One day I started losing my balance and it got worse."

"What causes it?" I inquired.

"My cerebellum just doesn't work, Wendy."

"Where is the cerebellum?"

She'd point to the back of her head. "It affects my equilibrium."

"What is equilibrium?"

"It has to do with my balance. It's in my spinal cord."

"Dr. Gorilla can give you more pills."

Mumma managed a smile, "Maybe. Maybe, if I'm lucky."

For a long time, I presumed that anyone who had MS was paralyzed, permanently bedridden, and would die from the disease like my mother. However, after I graduated from high school and moved to California, I was both surprised and relieved to learn that people who have the disease can often live a full and productive life.

As to be expected, it was difficult getting close to my mother, both emotionally and physically. Because her body was in a constant state of pain, physical closeness made it difficult for any snuggle time. But there was one indelible moment of mother-daughter connection. We were in the living room, the couch against the wall. I was young. I couldn't have been more than six or seven years old. My head rested in the crook of my mother's arm while Peppy, our dog, was nestled in between her legs. It was twilight. The sky was a mix of deep purples and blues. Mumma began to sing. It was the first memory I have of her singing. Her voice was soft, lilting, as she sang "How Much Is That Doggie in the Window." The lyrics made me smile. I glanced down at Peppy who was fast asleep. I felt safe cradled next to her. As the lullaby continued, "The one with the waggly tail," I gazed at the deeply saturated blues of the late evening sky while feeling the rise and fall of her chest.

As the song came to an end, she became quiet. I lifted my head and whispered, "Mumma, when will you die?" She tenderly brushed my hair with her non-crippled hand, "I won't leave you, Wendy...not until I know you're old enough to take care of yourself." I laid my head back in her arms. Those words were anchored forever in my sub-conscious. Then, she shifted her body position and lightened the mood by sharing a story about me as a toddler.

She had heard me crying and ran outside to find me tucked in the far corner of the playpen. A bee had stung me. I asked her if she had gotten stung by the bee, and she smiled and said no. Many a night I'd run that episode over in my mind: what it must've been like to have my mother 'run' outside, 'lift' me from the playpen, and 'rub' her hands over my bee-stung arm.

On another occasion, her warmer side emanated. We had an oil-burning stove in our living room. It had a small side door and my siblings and I often opened the door to take advantage of the fire's warmth. We stood as close as possible and Mumma yelled at us relentlessly to "shut the door." We didn't listen. The welcomed heat was worth the risk. Then one biting, frigid, winter evening, I suffered a significant burn on my knee. I bellowed in pain. "Mumma, Mumma," I cried. I grasped my knee and hobbled over to her. Mumma ordered Madeline, "Get some butter. Go!" Madeline dashed to the kitchen and returned with a stick of butter.

"Put your leg here, next to me." In between sobs, I lifted my leg and placed it on the couch near my mother's side.

She rubbed my knee with the stick of butter. Her hand was wobbly, but she kept ferociously lathering my knee with the Land O'Lakes butter stick. Afterward, she instructed Madeline to bring me to the bathroom, put iodine on it, and bandage my knee. I still bear that scar, and with it, the memory of Mumma giving her best effort to help her injured child.

Occasionally, Aunt Ruthie visited. To me, she and Mumma looked nearly identical. Same dark hair and features. I liked to sit close by as the two women smoked their cigarettes huddled together, sharing woman talk. Afterward, Aunt Ruthie hugged me and talked with me for a few moments, and then Mumma shooed me away, "Go to the bedroom." As I shuffled off, I noticed their conversations quieted to a whisper. I crouched on my knees in the hallway and tried to decipher what they were saying, but I never could.

Once my mother accidentally revealed an intimate childhood episode while she was consoling me after a rather tumultuous day at school. For the most part, I wasn't teased at school. I made friends fairly easily and got along with most everyone. Except once—I had a complete meltdown in the classroom. It was second grade. Mrs. Helen insisted that I stand up and read the story I was writing. I explained that I wasn't finished. She scolded me and demanded, "Stand up now and read it." I slowly stood up from my wooden desk.

Apparently, whatever I wrote wasn't up to standard. One kid chuckled, and then the rest of the class joined in. The boy directly in front of me made a funny face. My voice stuttered and anxiety overwhelmed me as I grappled to finish my story. As I struggled to speak, I felt my voice fading—like a car running out of gas and sputtering to a stop—until I ultimately was unable to speak at all. My voice just stopped working. I stood there feeling naked, embarrassed, and raw inside. The laughter grew louder and the room grew incredibly bright for me.

I dug deep and momentarily was able to speak again, "I can't see the words. I can't make 'em out." The classroom broke out in a blistering cacophony. Mrs. Helen warned the class to "settle down" and marched down the aisle, grabbed the sheet of paper, and mockingly said, "You can't read your own writing?" I collapsed in my chair and lay my head atop my arms, blocking my eyes with my arms, trying to stop the glaring light from penetrating. She escorted me out of the classroom. I spent the rest of the period in the principal's office, bewildered and ashamed.

I came home that afternoon utterly heartbroken. Mumma called me over to the couch where I sat next to her. I nestled my head in the crook of her arm and lay there with her. I asked, "Mumma, has anyone ever made fun of you?" She was quiet for a moment then shared in halting, broken sentences, "Hmm. Yeah. They called me a bastard." She was quiet again. I glanced up at her anguished face.

"What does bastard mean?" She raised an eyebrow, shook her head, and pulled her arm away. "It's just a bad word, Wendy. Never use it." She repositioned herself, and ordered, "Go get me some water." I jumped off the couch and ran to the kitchen sink, quietly repeating the word 'bastard' to myself as I turned on the faucet and filled the glass. The word resonated with me even as a youngster.

After the traumatic experience in second grade, I persevered and wrote my short stories. In fourth grade, I wrote a story called "The Growing Mustard Seed." I worked on it for hours and was particularly pleased with the line "My love for you is like a growing mustard seed." I counted the days until Mother's Day. That morning I went to Luty's flower shop and bought her a bouquet of flowers with my allowance money.

As with every Mother's Day, Mumma took great pleasure in singing "M-O-T-H-E-R: A Word that Means the World to Me" (lyrics by Howard E. Johnson, music by Theodore F. Morse). I beheld Mumma's bright look as she sang. We often joined in chorus with her. By now, she had a faded wart that looked more like a perpetual swollen blister on her upper lip. She was self-conscious of this protrusion, but when she sang, all her embarrassment disappeared. She was free and radiant in those sporadic, yet tender, song-filled moments.

"M" is for the million things she gave me
"O" means only that she's growing old
"T" is for the tears she shed to save me
"H" is for her heart of purest gold
"E" is for her eyes with love light shining
"R" means right and right she'll always be
Put them all together they spell MOTHER,
A word that means the world to me.

After we sang and my siblings left the room, I handed my mother the white, folded paper with a drawing of a sunflower on the front cover and her bouquet of flowers. I waited anxiously as she read my short story. She placed the paper on the TV tray. She was quiet. Said nothing. I held my breath. She didn't like it. The silence lasted an eternity when finally—she raised her head, intent on my face, her hazel-brown eyes penetrating my innermost self. She whispered, "I'm proud of you, Wendy."

Madeline, Jeff, Wendy and Kelly. My older brother Jeff was visiting during my sister's first communion. I seemed to have continually crooked bangs as a youth, circa 1971 or 1972.

Food Stamps and Social Workers

As a child I couldn't fully comprehend what being wards of the probate court of Gogebic County meant, but I knew it was serious and we had to behave. Social Services visited often. Like clockwork, before each social worker visit, Mumma made us clean the house and ensured we were well-groomed and wore our finest clothes. I was always on my best behavior when Mr. Kamny or Mr. Wilson came to call, as I was certain that if we misbehaved, I would be taken away from Mumma.

Regardless of this undercurrent of anxiety, I looked forward to the regular visits. The men were kind and offered encouraging words. I eagerly awaited to see which social worker drove up on visitation days. Bright-eyed and bushy-tailed, I dragged the yellow kitchen chair to the window and perched over the windowsill awaiting their arrival. After what seemed an eternity, a car pulled up and I strained to see who emerged from the car. I jumped down from the chair. "He's here, Mumma. He's here. It's Mr. Wilson." She nodded, "Keep it down. Behave."

Both of our social workers were kind men. But my favorite was Mr. Wilson. He visited with Mumma and asked her questions. Then he turned to us and, with a calm, relaxing smile, casually asked how we were doing. I felt like he really cared. And though his visit soothed me for the time being, I knew it was only a matter of time after he left, the angst and fear of being taken away would rear its ugly head again and inwardly torment me. I would go back to my usual routine.

Mumma was adamant about keeping the house clean even when the men from Social Services weren't visiting. We all had chores. And though we shared housecleaning duties of vacuuming, dusting, and scrubbing the floor, we each had a specific room that we were responsible for—my room was the bathroom. Every Sunday, we took turns taking our bath. Because we had no shower, in between bath days, we cleaned up with a wet rag and soap. Mumma was adamant that our necks and arms were clean. She inspected us afterward and told us, "You still have scurf on your neck, go wash." I trudged back into the bathroom and scrubbed my neck until all the dirt was gone. I emerged from the bathroom with a dazzling clean, albeit striking red neck from scrubbing.

I liked the smell of Spic and Span. I filled the mop bucket with warm water, poured in the cleaning solution, and dragged the heavy bucket down the short hallway. I took great pride in keeping the bathroom clean. I mopped the floor and fervently scrubbed the toilet with a rag and Comet. I was used to cleaning Mumma's bedpan and getting pee and poo on me, so I never minded a dirty toilet. The bathtub was different. There was a gap between the tub and the back wall, and I was convinced that mammoth spiders nested underneath the tub. I cleaned the front section of the bathtub heartily, but only gingerly touched the backside for fear one of those gigantic spiders would leap out and bite me.

Though bathroom cleaning was my main chore, filling out government forms on behalf of my mother was a top priority. We lived off food stamps and government assistance, and as a child it seemed to me that we consistently had to submit one kind of form or another. For some reason, Mumma pegged me to help her complete the forms. I don't recall how or when this task started, but I gathered it was because I received an A+ in penmanship classes.

I sat next to Mumma and she directed me on what to write on the forms. I made certain to write as neatly as possible. I truly believed if the handwriting wasn't legible, it would be a reason for the government to remove the children from the house. After I completed the forms, Mumma wrote her signature with her right hand. After a while however, that hand started to shake slightly, enough so, that her signature wasn't legible. I copied her signature for hours either at the kitchen table or on the bed. When I finally was convinced I had mastered the look of Mumma's signature, I proudly showed her, and she smiled and nodded.

Over the years I gained confidence that I performed this duty as Mumma's government document assistant quite well, not only because she praised me, but more importantly, because the food stamps and checks always arrived in the mail. In general, monies arrived on a Friday. I referred to them as Friday Fun Days.

In the 1970s, there were paper food stamps and I was fascinated by the colors and faces on the stamps. When they arrived, I insisted that I be the one to open the envelope. I got a kick out of tearing the stamps from the perforated binding. I liked the way the paper felt in my hands and the sound it made as I delicately ripped the sheets from the coupon book. In the early years, when it came to grocery shopping, however, it was Debbie who was responsible for carrying the food stamps to the grocery store because she was the oldest. She was careful not to lose them, knowing all too well it meant we wouldn't eat much that month. Grocery shopping was a joint effort done by the siblings, usually me and my two sisters. We took pen to paper and wrote down the list of items that Mumma instructed us to purchase. After the list was complete, we barreled out the door and rolled the red wagon off to the National Food Store or Carlson's Supermarket a few blocks from our house. In the winter months, we generally called for a taxi.

Grocery shopping was a high point in my chore list of things to do. I begged my sisters to let me pick out the treats while they did the main grocery shopping. When we entered the store, they went one way and I went the other. First order of business was getting the bag of yellow popcorn (which was about three feet tall). I dashed to the cookie aisle and picked out my favorites—Cracker Jacks, Barnum's Animals Crackers, and Oreo cookies. I then sauntered to the Brach's candy display and treated myself to a few candies. After finding my sisters, I showed them my treats and they either vetoed them or allowed me to dump them in the cart. More often than not, they then would have to remind me to "Go get Mumma's cigarettes."

I played a game with myself when I shopped for

Mumma's Pall Mall cigarettes. I picked the carton at the bottom of the tall stack of cigarettes to see if I could pull out the red box and not have the other cartons topple over. I became rather proficient at this grocery store entertainment.

If they still had a lot of grocery shopping to do, I meandered throughout the store. I played at the entry and exit area and hung upside down on the silver rails near the mega-sized bags of dog food and the bubble gum machines. I enjoyed wandering the vegetable and fruit section and was fascinated by the various colors and shapes of produce. I visited the butchers in the meat section or played hopscotch on the dark-green-and-white checkered floor.

As my sisters got close to finishing the shopping, I sprinted to the frozen section and picked out the family's frozen treats. There was great deliberation on this major life choice of either Neapolitan ice cream, Fudgsicles, Pushups, or Popsicles.

We rolled up to the checkout stands with an overflowing grocery cart. The clerks were so friendly. I studied their hands as they darted across the cash register keys. I liked to help bag the groceries. I pleaded with my sisters to let me pay. I methodically counted the stamps and handed the brightly colored sheets to the clerk.

Even better than the arrival of food stamps was when the state check came in the mail. That check meant burgers for supper. Mumma liked her hamburger well done with lots of fried onions. One or two of us jumped on our bikes, headed off to the bank, cashed the check, then hurried off to Bridgeman's, a local diner in downtown Ironwood. The other special treat—Bismarck doughnuts from Carlson's Supermarket, which was across the street. I relished every bite of the jelly-filled doughnuts. Mumma's face lit up as she bit into her custard-filled doughnut. I could tell these Friday meals made her happy. If it wasn't burgers, she treated us to pasties from Joe's pasty shop. Pasties were my favorite—far more delicious than the burger. I dream about visiting Ironwood to this day and making a pasty run.

In between the bigger grocery store runs, one of us had to make the trek to the store for milk, bread, eggs, or cigarettes. When I was old enough, Mumma asked me to go to the store and get her a carton of her Pall Malls and a loaf of Wonder Bread. I stood obediently at the foot of the couch and studied the twenty-dollar bill as she lectured me on the importance of keeping the money safely in my pocket. I was thrilled that she thought I was responsible to carry this amount of cash.

And so, I trotted off to the store. The morning was sunny. I could take a shortcut up the knoll through the grove of trees. But during the late spring months, I preferred to go up the sidewalk on McLeod Street where the hefty lilac bush sprawled for half of the block.

I shoved my face in the fresh sweetness of the purple buds then continued on my walk as I gazed at the sun filtering through the towering trees. I sauntered along in my reverie and, upon arriving at the store, I was alarmed to discover that I lost the twenty-dollar bill. I was devastated. How could I tell Mumma? I was petrified to go home.

I dawdled back to the house and eventually got the nerve and quietly pushed open the front door. I couldn't hide. The couch was right there at the entrance. I hoped she was sleeping. She wasn't.

Shaking, I said, "Mumma, I lost the money."

She screeched, "That's all we have until next month!" She scowled and glared at me with those steely, hazel-brown eyes. "Did you steal the money?"

"No!" I cried.

"You won't get your allowance all month."

"I can go back and keep looking," I begged.

"No, you won't. Go to your room, you're grounded."

I hung my head and dragged my feet into the bedroom. Kelly was fast asleep on the bigger bed and so I curled up on the rollaway with our blue, lightweight, Snoopy blanket and fell asleep. Later that evening, I sat on the bed and gazed at a red robin skitter on a nearby tree limb as a few of my other siblings played a game of tag.

It took a while for me to earn Mumma's trust and convince her that I could be responsible with cash.

Wendy sits on Madeline's shoulders while Kelly plays on Greg's back. July 1974.

Purple Taxi

Our feet and our bikes were our modes of transportation—that is, until laundry days, and then we called a taxi. There were several taxis to choose from, but our favorite was Virgil's Cab Company, which was located down the street from our property. He knew our family well, and Mumma liked him, too.

I liked doing the laundry, but only in the summer months. I dreaded doing laundry in the winter. Tens of inches of snow could fall overnight, and so before doing laundry, I pulled out the snow scoop, which was twice my size, and shoveled a path from the front door to the street, a chore I loathed. I put on three pairs of socks, wrapped my feet in Wonder Bread bags, slipped on my snow boots, donned my parka and gloves, and then ventured out into the blistering cold. The first few yards were toughest. Using all my strength, I picked up the burly, rusted, silver snow scoop, shoved it downwards, and then pushed and pushed, all the while trying to find a place to dump the white powder without blocking the path. I didn't have much choice. It was either shoveling, or carrying heavy laundry baskets while sinking into waist-high snow. With the coming of summer, my heightened enthusiasm for laundry days emerged.

A lot of children meant a lot of dirty laundry. Once a week, we emptied the hamper and filled up the plastic baskets. I got a thrill making the phone call to Patricia, who worked at Virgil's. She often picked up the phone and I adored her sense of humor as she made me laugh. "Is it that time again, Wendy?" "Yep," I'd say. "See you in a jiffy," she quipped.

I'd hang up the phone and sit on the mountain of clothes, anxiously awaiting the arrival of the purple taxi. Either Virgil or Patricia picked us up. They helped carry the baskets to and from the car.

My siblings and I hopped in the back seat, nestled in between the baskets. As the taxi tumbled along the roadway onto Highway 2 where the laundromat was located, I rested my head on the basket while Patricia smoked her cigarettes and shared amusing tales about strange customers she had driven that week. Her stories either made me afraid or made me laugh, and time and again, captivated my imagination.

I liked to load the clothes into the washers and put the coins in the slot. My sisters constantly reminded me to not stuff the clothes, but I didn't understand. If I loaded more clothes in the washer, that meant fewer washing machines and less money. As soon as they turned their backs, I shoved as many clothes as I could inside the tub. Then I gingerly placed the coins in their respective slots and pushed the coin handles in.

While we waited for the clothes to wash and dry, we sat on the huge, faded-blue folding table and did homework or played a card game of Crazy Eights. During the summer months, we sprinted across the street to the Indianhead

Motel and explored the grounds. On those frosty winter days, I eagerly waited to pull the hot clothes out of the dryer and immerse my head in the warmth of the clothes. What I didn't like, however, was folding the clothes. I often disappeared outside and let my siblings fold. Other times I ran off to the bathroom and read a magazine. I timed it just right; when the clothes were almost all folded, I sauntered back over to the blue table and folded the remaining few.

During one laundry excursion, I forgot the box of Tide at the laundromat. As we were exiting the taxi, I gasped. Madeline asked what was wrong. I lied and said nothing, but I knew Mumma would be mad, so I jumped on my red, white, and blue banana bike, and rode the two-mile trek back up Cloverland Drive to the laundromat. To my dismay, the box of detergent was no longer there. Panic set in. What to do? I hopped on the bike and peddled to the National Food Store and picked up a box of Tide using my allowance money. But first, I snuck out to the back of the store, opened the box, and dumped detergent by some dilapidated, rusty, grocery carts, and then buried the detergent under an empty, moldy, vegetable box.

I wasn't riding my usual bike which had a basket in the front. Instead, I balanced the open box of Tide on my handlebars, and lost my balance in front of Kaufman's Store. I swerved just as a motorcycle was barreling down Aurora Street. The man accidentally hit my back tire. I went flying, and so did the detergent!

The man quickly dismounted his bike and dashed to my aid. Despite the crash landing, I was okay. He asked where

I lived. I pointed to the dirt road, which ran along the side of our property.

He noted that I was a bit stunned and gently picked me up from the ground. I blurted out, "We can't leave without the Tide." He raised an eyebrow, but I insisted. He gingerly placed me back on the ground, sauntered over to the now busted open container. I grabbed it from him and clutched tightly to the box and the remains of detergent. With child and Tide in hand, he carried me the few hundred feet down the dirt road.

Before entering the house, I dropped the box of Tide next to the outside steps. Mumma was beside herself wondering who this man was, carrying her daughter. He placed me on the oversized green chair. He was a gracious man and put our family at ease, especially Mumma. He explained what happened, as I was shook up. I assured everyone that I was okay and didn't need to go to the hospital.

Later that night, I lay in bed gazing out the window at the colorful northern lights as they dazzled and lit up the pitch-dark skies. I was banged up with a broken bike, but pleased that I clandestinely and successfully brought home the box of detergent.

The following morning while I was emptying Mumma's bedpan, I heard a knock on the door. Who could that be so early? Greg opened the door, and I poked my head around the corner. It was Patty. "Hi, everyone, just wanted to return this box of Tide. I think you left it in the taxi."

Shirley and Louie Sr., my dad, two years into their marriage.
May 18, 1951.

Bessemer Brothers

Mumma often told the story about when she and my dad were married and lived in Bessemer. One evening, as she descended deep into the basement, a rat "as big as a dog" lunged at her. This tale frightened me every time she described it. I figured the rat was as big as our dog Peppy— he was at least 45 pounds. While Mumma was in the mood to share tales about the past, I questioned her about Dad. Who was he? What type of man was he? According to Mumma—he was no good. He left her. Period. I took her at her word.

Dad never stepped inside our house in Ironwood except for one time. I don't think Mumma appreciated his presence. Normally, he dropped off the boys so they could visit Mumma or their siblings. On this isolated visit, he called ahead of time and informed Mumma he needed to bring some documents by for her to sign. "Why don't you just leave the papers with the boys?" she yelled into the phone.

I asked her what the paper was that she needed to sign, but she only glared at me. I shrugged my shoulders, then asked if she wanted me to sign the documents for her, as I did the other documents that we sent to the state. She furrowed her brow, "I need to sign it myself; go to your room." I never did find out what the paper was she needed to sign. It was obvious she wasn't thrilled about his visit. End of discussion.

The days leading up to his visit, Mumma yammered on and on about our father, reminding us every chance she could that he was a lousy man. I sensed she was anxious, but I wasn't exactly sure why. On the day of his visit, I was concerned about Dad entering the house. Mumma never spoke fondly of him, so how would she act—would she yell at him? Much to my surprise, Mumma made an all-out effort to look attractive. The night before, she had us put the plastic pink curlers in her bangs. The morning of, we bathed her, we dressed her with a fresh hospital gown. We propped up the pillows as usual, so she could sit up as straight as she could on the couch.

Expecting the worst, I was bewildered to hear a soft knock on the door. Dad entered. My brothers, Greg and Randy, dashed in behind him. From behind his thick glasses, Dad scanned our small living room with his penetrating, dark-brown, Italian eyes.

He was all business and barely uttered a word. There was a quick hello between my mother and father. Dad nodded to her, and she nodded in return. He sized up my mother's bedridden body, covered by a lightweight, jade blanket. She pulled the blanket up past her waist and mustered strength to sit straighter in the bed, a task that was difficult for her.

He laid the paper on the TV tray. She skimmed the paper then asked me to get her the pen. She scrawled her signature with her shaky hand, and then tossed the pen aside. Dad picked up the sheet of paper and tucked it in his coat pocket. He didn't stay long and said he'd return to pick the boys up at the end of the weekend. He left as quietly as he came.

What I remember most about the visit was the look of both sadness and disdain between my dad and mother; it was as if there were stories between them that only they shared. He knew her from another time, back when she was vibrant and full of life, and here she was now a broken woman tethered to a green couch. Pity overrode animosity. I could tell she was embarrassed. She appeared relieved when he left.

I suspect this feeling of shame is why Mumma didn't have a whole lot of visitors. Occasionally, relatives and friends stopped by—Bootsie, her boisterous cousin, or our truck-driving uncle swung by when in town and shared stories of his travels across the United States, Charlie and Florence Volkman paid a visit, or our neighbor Laverne, or our Aunt Ruthie and her husband, Nelson. In the earlier years, her confidant Mary July visited. Mumma's face lit up with excitement seeing her good friend. But Mary's visits became fewer and fewer. I suspect that Mumma didn't appreciate prying eyes, even though I was under the impression that the visitors brought a ray of sunshine to our house. She felt ashamed, as if they were judging her. Perhaps they were. She never said it in so many words, but shame was there—a steady, pulsating, undercurrent in our family life.

I often wondered what life would be like with my dad. I wished to be close to him and get to know my other brothers. Once, I asked Mumma if I could spend the summer in Bessemer, and she flat-out said 'no'; and yet again, reminded me how he left her and was unreliable. I never asked again and learned to appreciate occasional weekend visits with my dad.

A simple, quiet town about six miles from Ironwood, Bessemer was nestled alongside picturesque bluffs, and served as the county seat of Gogebic County. Since we never had a car, I eagerly enjoyed any chance I could to ride in a car, and most especially, the car ride to Bessemer with my dad. Dad's car was massive, like a fortress of steel.

As we ventured along Highway 2, I stuck my head out the window and let the wind whip my hair and face. I reveled when, instead of taking the highway, we drove the back roads to the Fairview Apartments, where he resided. In the autumn months, tree limbs dangled their lush golden, red, and yellow leaves across the rural stretch of road as we traveled the winding roadway.

Without fail, Dad instructed us to lock the car doors. On a particular stretch of winding road, he recounted a tale when Greg fell out of the car. He pointed, "Right there. Your brother bounced off the pavement, like a basketball. Landed there by that tree." I peered over the car window at the fast-moving, gray concrete then cautiously moved away from the car door toward the center. Years later, Dad divulged that "Actually, Randy pushed Greg out the door." The two youngsters were playing in the back seat and Greg went flying out the door. Dad was never certain if it was an accident or on purpose. Thankfully, Dad was driving slowly and Greg wasn't severely injured.

During the visitation weekends, Dad drove us to his mother's house. I cherished those weekend visits with my Italian grandmother. She was born in northern Italy. I didn't visit her often, yet enjoyed her lighthearted nature, especially when she was conversing in her native tongue. I relished her homemade gnocchi. Once, I asked Mumma if we could have gnocchi for dinner, and she scoffed, "We don't make that in this house." I never asked again.

By 1974, six of the ten siblings were living with Mumma. Ricky and Louie were well past the age of eighteen and were no longer living at home, so it was just Jeff and Randy living with my dad.

Dad's apartment was an end unit and nestled up to dense, forested hills. While a majority of kids explored the Bessemer bluffs and rambled along the rounded cliffs that bordered the town, I was content swinging on the mega swing set on the expansive play yard a short distance from Dad's apartment complex. What I enjoyed about Fairview Apartments is that there were lots of children to play with. Unlike Ironwood, where our dwelling sat some distance from the street and was surrounded by trees, the Fairview apartments were clusters of buildings, paved streets imprinted with chalk-colored hopscotch squares, and kids peddling to and fro on their bicycles, with as many kids as you could fit on the banana bike's front and back fenders. Summertime in Bessemer was a flurry of festive fun. Dad would be in the apartment making spaghetti, and the rest of us were left to our own devices in the great outdoors.

My brother Jeff was more of a woodsy guy—creative, talented, and skilled at building things. On one visit, he showed me the bunny rabbit cages he built in close proximity to the edge of the woods at the rear side of the apartments. As he proudly gave me the bunny cage tour, I noticed one cage was empty. I pointed and asked, "Where's that bunny rabbit?" Jeff chuckled and said, "We ate that one. Made rabbit stew." I cried, "You can't eat them!" He laughed, "Only teasing," ruffled my hair, and sauntered off. In truth, I don't think he was teasing.

Randy was one year older than me and he teased and tormented me often. He had a penchant for causing mischief. But one hot, muggy, Midwestern summer afternoon, his mischief turned malicious. I was playing hopscotch out front of Dad's apartment near the jumbo storage building when, seemingly out of nowhere, Randy rode up behind me on his bicycle and knocked me to the ground. But that wasn't enough—instead of riding off, he rode his bicycle on top of me. My blouse got stuck in the chain, and unable to go anywhere, Randy leapt off the bike and abandoned me there on the hot, gray pavement. Needless to say, I screamed and cried at the top of my lungs. A few folks ran over, including my dad. While pinned under the bike, one person held it up over my body as Dad ripped my favorite purple shirt, freeing me from the greasy bike chain.

For all my fun-filled frolic and occasional frightful visits to Bessemer, I was ecstatic when Jeff and Randy spent the weekend in Ironwood. First, it meant we had additional people to play tag; second, it made the game of "Statue" livelier, and finally, hide-and-seek was more challenging as my Bessemer brothers inevitably found new places to hide.

I could tell Mumma was delighted having her sons visit. All the same, her wrath could bring out her beastly side.

During a weekend while Randy visited us, I was cleaning the bathroom, and as I proceeded down the short, dimly lit hallway to empty the bucket, Randy leapt out from a crawl space under the storage shelves. Startled, I screeched, and the bucket of water went flying. Mumma wasn't happy and wouldn't let either of us play outside. I was mad that I got blamed for something that my brother did to me. Mumma sent all of us, including my brothers and sisters, to bed without supper.

We huddled in our beds with the lights out and had one of our fantasy feasts. I was accustomed to these pretend meals, but for Randy, it was a first-time experience. We took turns sharing what we were 'eating.' I devoured a gargantuan bowl of peaches with whipped cream and Fig Newtons; another sibling had a pork chop smothered with Shake 'n Bake. Yet another even hungrier sibling, imagined a grilled cheese sandwich and a Swanson's TV dinner, while another envisioned a hearty meal of Hamburger Helper and Chef Boyardee Ravioli. These imaginary banquets kept us entertained and, quite honestly, it helped me not to feel so hungry. But these imaginative dinners didn't work for Randy. He was not used to this going-to-bed-with-no-food punishment.

Mumma was living in the other bedroom during this period. She was listening to one of her favorite records "Shoes," sung by Patsy Kline (over and over, as she often did). Randy was feeling brave and snuck out of the bedroom, crawled on his belly into the kitchen, and proudly returned displaying his conquest—the butter dish! He removed the plastic top and licked the half stick of softened butter. He offered me a bite. It tasted disgusting. He chuckled, scooped a fingerful of butter and shoved it in his mouth. We gagged and dared him to eat the whole thing. Spurred on by the challenge, he then proceeded to eat the remaining stick of butter. After Randy's butter feast entertainment, we retreated to bed, usually three to a bed; all jockeying for our space on the double bed. As usual, as I drifted to sleep I awoke to a kick in the face by one of my siblings as they rolled over.

When Jeff spent the night, he got a kick from sharing a tale that chilled me to the bone. Now mind you, I often sat close to Mumma while she watched "Night Gallery," because the TV show frightened her. I kept her company while I hid my head under a blanket or closed my eyes. But as scary as her horror shows were, nothing was ghastlier than the tale titled "The Velvet Ribbon." As the story goes, a woman married a man, and on their honeymoon, she warned him to never remove the green velvet ribbon she perpetually wore around her neck. He promised. Well, that promise was short-lived, and he grew obsessed with that green ribbon. When finally, one evening at the stroke of midnight he snuck into her room and removed the green velvet, and her head fell off and, as it rolled onto the floor, she bellowed, "I told you that you'd be sorrrrrrryyyyyy." I followed Jeff's face closely as he delighted in scaring me while he recounted that frightful tale. Inevitably, those nights I lay awake too afraid to move. I touched my neck to ensure it was safe, then pulled the blankets up over my head.

Of all my seven brothers, Louie was the most mysterious to me. Born in 1949, he was fourteen years older than I was. Mumma frequently spoke so affectionately of him and was proud of the young man he had become. He, like all of my brothers, was good-looking. He had the same dark-brown hair like my other brothers, and soothing brown eyes were hidden behind his glasses. His picture hung on our living room wall close to the sizeable, black-framed painting of wild horses running in a vast, barren landscape, overshadowed by ominous clouds. Every now and again, Mumma pointed to Louie's photo and reminded us how smart our oldest brother was, and she hoped that we grew up to be as bright as him.

Louie went to Vietnam and periodically visited us after the war. Unlike Ricky's carefree, lighthearted self, Louie was quiet and reserved. He seemed deep in thought, and much like that visit with my dad, Louie and Mumma's conversations were much shorter than the ones she had with Ricky, but it seemed to me there was a silent understanding between them. I felt as if he and Mumma shared a stormy and veiled history together. Even as a child, I could never put my finger on it; only she acted differently around him— well-behaved, softer, meeker.

After their short conversations, Louie ride, often to Dairy Queen. I climbed into seat making sure I sat right behind him.

along, I noted his short-cropped hair, intrigued by how his glasses rested on his ears. It fascinated me how a person could maneuver a car by merely moving the steering wheel with their hands. When we turned a corner, I followed Louie's hands closely as they alternated over each other. Once, I sat in the front seat and asked him if it was scary to drive, and he chuckled, shook his head 'no,' and accelerated, pushing on the gas pedal. My heart skipped a beat. Exhilarated, I gripped the door handle as we flew down the highway.

Louie had a giant album collection. It ran the length of the wall on a low, narrow shelf. When I visited, he proudly showed it off. He asked me what I listened to. I shrugged—Mumma never asked us what music we enjoyed, and she rarely listened to rock-n-roll. She was a country music woman: Johnny Cash, Roy Clark, Patsy Cline, Loretta Lynn, Tammy Wynette, and Dolly Parton among her favorites. "You choose," I said. He pulled an album from the shelf and held it up so I could see the cover. I chuckled at the name "Deep Purple." He slid the disc from its sleeve, placed it on the record player, and then took a seat on the red velvet couch. He tapped his foot and nodded his head in tempo. His eyes glazed over—spellbound by the music. As the melody enveloped him, I joined in with him swaying side to side on the plush sofa. I felt safe and secure. The pulsating bass was too strong to resist.

Because he was older than me, I hadn't hung out with Louie. He was on his own by the time Mumma was permanently bedridden. Although we had the same mother,

I knew her when she was confined to her bed, while Louie had known Mumma when she was able-bodied, led some other life, and was a different person. I often wondered what stories he could tell about my mother when she was footloose and fancy-free. I always wanted to ask him, "What was it like when Mumma walked?" But I never did.

Though I was unable to get as close to my brothers in Bessemer as I desired, I continued to look up to them. There were moments I wished I could have lived with them and Dad, especially on those days when Mumma was anything but kind.

My siblings spent Christmas in Bessemer, Michigan. Back left to right. Ricky, Madeline (newborn), Louie, Debbie with her doll, Jeff, Johnny. December 1960.

White Bag of Pills

Although there was never alcohol in our house, Mumma had plenty of pill bottles on her TV tray tucked in between the ashtray, cigarettes, TV Guide, and cups of coffee. When my mother had MS there weren't many disease-modifying therapies. In the 1960s, doctors were just beginning to understand the immune system's role in MS. The medical community cycled between treating MS with antibiotics or immune suppressants, depending on what theory was prevalent at the time. The oral medications to treat the surface symptoms were often painkillers, sedatives, oral steroids, or amphetamines, which were perceived to potentially help with the pain, fatigue, numbness, and other symptoms that accompanied MS. Nothing in the arsenal of pills and drugs the doctors prescribed treated the underlying disease.

Dr. Gorilla was our family doctor and made periodic visits. At almost every visit, he dropped off a prescription. We joked at how anyone could read Dr. Gorilla's handwriting. I was a curious and determined child. One evening, I spent hours trying to decipher the letters on the prescription sheet to no avail. On the next pharmacy run, I asked the pharmacist how they could read his scribble. The pharmacist chuckled, "We have a secret code for doctors' handwriting." I had no reason to doubt him. "What pills does my mother get?" He studied the paper, peered up from his eyeglasses, smiled, and quipped, "Pills that will make her feel better." Obviously, I wasn't going to get an answer, and it wouldn't have mattered what information they conveyed. Bottom line, Mumma needed her pills. It wasn't uncommon to have Mumma call Dr. Gorilla. She'd get off the phone and say, "Go pick up a prescription."

Truth is, I liked getting her pills—it got me out of the house. On occasion, Greg and I went to the pharmacy together. On our way we stopped at McLellan's to get a banana split. McLellan's had a customer game at their lunch counter. Balloons hung on long strings from the ceiling. Inside each balloon was a slip of paper that listed the price a customer would pay for their banana split.

Greg and I eagerly took our seats. I was giddy with anticipation as the waitress plucked a balloon, popped it, and revealed the little-bitty slip of paper. For good luck, I crossed my fingers, my legs, and my arms hoping for a free banana split. Much to my delight, the waitress sometimes let us pop the balloon.

More often than not, it was just me who did the pill run. Prescription slip in my hand, I hopped on my bike and headed off to the pharmacy. In early-to-mid-1970s, Ironwood had a population of approximately 8,000 and there were a few pharmacies. Between the Apothecary, Trier's, Walgreens, and Ironwood Pharmacy on South Suffolk Street, I preferred the latter, mainly because it was across the street from Hulstrom's City News and Agate Shop, aka "The Candy Store." Upon entering the pharmacy, the pharmacists happily greeted me. I handed over the prescription and, after sharing pleasantries of how my mother was, I wandered off to the magazine aisle and digested articles and photos from *Teen Beat*, *Seventeen*, *People*, and other celebrity magazines. On more than one occasion, I was so lost in my world, the pharmacist delivered the prescription to me while I was stretched out on the floor surrounded by magazines.

More often, however, as soon as I handed over the white slip of paper with illegible writing, I trotted across the street to the candy store. The country store had a mish-mash of everything imaginable, and then some. Upon entering this treasured getaway, I zeroed in on the candy section. The counter and the display cases filled up the whole front section of the store and were stuffed with an assortment of sugary goodness. I purchased the usual soft and chewy, red licorice rope, a bubble gum cigar, candy cigarettes, Pop Rocks, Charleston Chews, Bazooka Bubble Gum, and a candy charm necklace. After reading Bazooka Joe's comic strip, I wandered through the store chewing on my candy cigar.

I studied the intricate wooden signs, the colorful agates mainly retrieved from Lake Superior, and more often than not, managed to make my way to an abundant collection of magazines that spanned the entire wall of the store. If I was feeling brave, I snuck a peek at the X-rated magazines, then sauntered over to the celebrity magazine section. Hulstrom's had a much larger selection of magazines than the pharmacy. I picked my favorites, plopped on the floor, and was soon transported in a reverie of celebrity crushes—Tony Orlando, Tom Jones, or Paul Michael Glaser, "Starsky."

Eventually, I made it home, and Mumma asked what took so long. I invariably lied and said, "Don't know. Just took a while to fill the prescription." I don't think she minded just as long as I returned with the white bag. I don't know what the pills were, but I know Mumma needed them—and she liked them. During one visit, Dr. Gorilla notified Mumma there were ground-breaking drugs on the market for MS. He scribbled on the white piece of paper and, as expected, casually dropped it on her TV tray. After he left, I volunteered to get the prescription. Mumma took the pills, but nothing changed. She was still paralyzed and still in constant pain.

With all our repeated visits to the pharmacy, we knew the pharmacists quite well, so you can imagine the embarrassment when my brother Ricky and his friend were arrested for burglary at the pharmacy. Mumma was horrified and overwhelmed with anxiety that he could go to jail. But it wasn't the first time Ricky was in trouble.

Of all my siblings, I felt Mumma favored Ricky the most, and yet he caused her the greatest distress. I looked forward to Ricky's occasional visits. He was a boisterous and playful brother. He and Mumma smoked their cigarettes and chatted. When they were done talking, Ricky played with me. When I was younger and smaller, he picked me up and twirled me around. He wrestled me to the ground and sat on top of me and tickled me until my ribs hurt from laughing so hard. I squealed with delight, and Ricky tickled me that much harder. Even as I matured, Ricky loved to kid around. He told jokes and ruffled my hair. He was fun to be around. He brought vibrancy and merriment to our household.

But for all his fun-loving side, Ricky had a penchant for getting into trouble. It seemed alcohol was the problem. I heard one heated conversation between Mumma and Ricky. It had to do with alcohol and the difficulties it caused him. I sat at the kitchen table pretending to do my homework as they quarreled. At the end of the argument, Ricky smashed out his cigarette, got up from the couch, and headed for the kitchen. "Don't drink, Ricky. That alcohol causes problems," Mumma implored. "Don't worry, Ma. I can handle it," Ricky quipped. He glanced at me and winked as he opened the fridge and took a big gulp from the milk container.

She was so proud of him when he enrolled in the Marines in Spring 1973, but that all changed quickly—he went AWOL. Mumma was beside herself. I didn't understand all the details, but I recognized something was definitely not right. Even the FBI got involved. Then one day a man came to our house wearing a military uniform. I hid next to the fridge, tucked in the corner of the kitchen by the window, while he visited Mumma. It was serious—Ricky forged separation papers. After he left, Mumma was distraught. She was literally shaking as she smoked cigarette after cigarette while lamenting over how her son could do this.

During the period they were trying to locate my brother, Mumma talked endlessly about him, and if he was dishonorably discharged, what shame that would bring to the family. It didn't matter to me. He was my brother; but apparently, it was frowned upon to be dishonorably discharged. Ricky was eventually apprehended and for reasons I do not remember, he did not receive a dishonorable discharge. My mother and Ricky were pleased with this decision.

But his tribulations did not stop there. Ricky was a jokester, full of laughs and, in July of 1974, the song, "The Streak," was at the top of the charts. My twenty-two-year-old brother decided it would be a brilliant idea to streak at a softball tournament in Bessemer. With a "big box of popular chewing gum" in hand (according to the papers), he dashed along the bases in full-frontal glory. Apparently, a lot of streaking arrests were made that year. Unfortunately, my brother's incident made the local newspapers, and Mumma was, once again, distressed.

She lamented the perils of alcohol while smoking her cigarettes. I felt sorry for my brother—it seemed he did a lot of foolish things while under the influence. But the most distressing news was when he and his partying friend were arrested for breaking into the Ironwood Pharmacy on February 17, 1975. They were apprehended in the pharmacy after entering through a window. While he was detained in the Bessemer County jail, many family conversations centered around the prison to which Ricky might be sent. Mumma was concerned that he'd be sent far away. Even if he were sentenced closer, it wouldn't have mattered; Mumma was housebound on the green couch, and we didn't have a car. Nonetheless, this period of my life was tense; not only was my mother in a heightened state of anxiety, but I was losing my brother. On August 27,

1975, he was sentenced to one-and-one-half-to-four-years at a correctional facility in Ionia, located in the Lower Peninsula about an eight-hour bus ride away. This was an eternity in my child mind.

While serving his prison sentence the hit song "Tie a Yellow Ribbon Round the Ole Oak Tree" by Tony Orlando and Dawn was holding steady at the top of the charts. When that song came on the radio, Mumma directed us to turn it up. Other times, she'd have us put the 45 on the record player, and she listened to that song for hours. She called us to assist her with lighting her cigarette and then asked us to give her one of the pills from a pill bottle. Then Mumma shooed us away and gazed out the window.

I scrutinized my mother as her lips mounted the cigarette as she took deep puffs, with that faraway look in her eyes. It was as if she was physically in bed, but her mind was elsewhere—transported to a happier period of life. As she exhaled the smoke, my eyes followed the misty vapor rise toward the light of the window and dissolve into nothingness.

Wendy sports a flower-powered 1970s outfit. Johnny stands in front of our house on Norfolk Street, Ironwood, Michigan. Summer 1976.

The Fire

As a result of being a child caregiver, one imprinted life lesson was just how significant health is—the ability to stand, to walk, go to the bathroom unassisted, prepare simple meals, shower, or bathe—I never took these life activities for granted. Every now and again, I pondered if my mother was sad or upset that she could no longer go outside and feel the warmth of the summer sun on her body, smell the blossoming lilac bush in the spring, go on a car ride to Lake Superior, or swim at Norrie Park. Some nights when I lay in bed with my sister Debbie or Madeline, I heard my mother whimper in pain in the living room. This weighed on me. I prayed to God that He would help Mumma walk again.

Yet there were other times when I was tired of her asking me to give her the bedpan or bathe her. "Why do I have to? Can't Debbie or Madeline?" I stomped my foot or sighed heavily, grabbed the silver stainless steel bedpan and shoved it under her bum. On my way to the bathroom, I inevitably felt guilty and, as I dumped the remains in the toilet bowl, reminded myself, 'She can't help it, Wendy. Get over it.'

In my younger years, I assumed what we were dealing with as a family was typical. But as I grew up and classmates or teachers asked how our mother was doing, I came to realize that our situation wasn't the norm. I saw parents at school or at the grocery store with their children, and I privately wondered how Mumma felt that she couldn't attend school events, go to the bank, or shop at the grocery store. Did she miss cleaning the house, doing the laundry, cooking—all those routine duties that unite a family?

One evening, there was a polka festival at the American Legion Memorial Building, aka the Memorial Building. Greg and I pleaded with Mumma to let us go. She wouldn't agree at first; but Greg and I were a united force and just kept begging. Finally, Mumma relented, but demanded that we be home by a certain hour. We promised, jumped on our bikes, and zoomed up McLeod Street. That sultry, muggy evening was special for me. I learned how to polka. They closed off a portion of the streets for the festivities. It was a bustle of energy. The streetlights shimmered as we grabbed hands, twirled with our partners, and allowed the music to guide us from side to side with a hop-step-close-step over and over near the intersection of East McLeod Avenue and Marquette Street. I exhausted myself. Dripping with sweat, I sat on the concrete steps of the Memorial Building, took a much-needed rest break, and happily checked out folks of all ages shimmy and sway. I thought of Mumma. Did she ever go to a polka party?

It was nightfall by the time the crowds dispersed and the band broke for the evening. Greg and I rode our bikes the half-mile, quiet stretch from the Memorial Building to our meager tin-roofed hut singing "roll out the barrel, we'll have a barrel of fun" at the top of our lungs. Mumma was up waiting for us; everyone else, fast asleep. She was lost in another world watching Frankenstein on TV. Excited, we described the night's festivities. I asked Mumma if she knew how to polka. Preoccupied more with the exploits of Frankenstein's conquests, she quickly nodded and ushered us off to bed.

Exhausted, I collapsed onto the bed beside my sister Madeline who was already fast asleep and who, as usual, managed to hog the entire bed. I nudged her, wanting to tell her all about the evening. She didn't move. Instead, she started into her almost nightly routine of rolling her head side to side, back and forth for hours. I lay there, the music fresh in my head, and contemplated why my sister rolled her head. Was she dreaming? Did she have nightmares like I did and never spoke of them? Eventually, I settled into my corner of the bed, rolled over, and was fast asleep.

Our tiny 450-square-foot dwelling at 308 West McLeod Street didn't go unnoticed by our social workers. Brand-new public housing was being built in the early 1970s, and our family was fortunate to be on the list of applicants. When we heard that our application was accepted, we were beyond ecstatic. No longer would we have to squeeze three or four in a bed, we would actually have four bedrooms and two bathrooms. Imagine our excitement. I was further excited because our accommodations would be closer to Hiawatha Park, where Greg and I often played a game of "Bonnie and Clyde" in and around the caboose.

It was 1974 when we moved to the spacious, never-before-lived-in house on South Norfolk Street. The dark-brown, split-level house was about a half mile from the Quonset hut. It had a mustard yellow front door and window trim, a basement, and a garage sporting the same dark yellow. Even though we didn't have a vehicle, we were grateful to have this additional space for storage.

Madeline and I shared a room, and I had my own bed. I was in heaven. Agnes, our social service caretaker, continued to stop in a few days a week to clean and cook her fabulous meals. The green couch followed us, and Mumma took up residence initially in one of the bedrooms, and then eventually she and the green sofa moved into the living room where she could keep her usual eagle eye on us. We all adapted quickly to our new living arrangements. We had a mammoth back yard. In the summer months, the neighborhood kids got together and played kickball or softball in the expansive common space that connected all the parcels. It was heavenly to have all this open space, freedom, and kids to play with.

It was June 7, 1975, when the bubble burst. It was a mild, overcast day. I was on my bed listening to Olivia Newton-John on Casey Kasem's America's Top 40. His radio show was a weekly ritual for me. While listening, I was fixing a broken cassette tape of songs I had recorded off the radio. As I was taping the two broken ends of brown plastic film together with scotch tape, Madeline screamed, "Get out! Now!" I tossed the cassette aside, sprung from the bed, and made a quick escape. There was a billow of smoke coming from the back bedroom. I peered around the corner to check out the cause of the commotion only to witness a giant flame burst from the closet area. I panicked. We all panicked. I ran toward the living room to behold my otherwise stoic mother completely terrified.

She had thrown the covers off her body, desperately trying to move, but was unable to lift her body. I ran to her and propped her up. Madeline sprang into action, and with what seemed like super-human strength, she picked up our frail mom, and carried her outside to the street.

Firefighters were quick to respond. The fire was caused by a faulty electrical outlet. The stench of smoke saturated

Fires Doused

Two fires were quenched by Ironwood fire fighters Friday afternoon, one a case of arson.

Three firemen were called to Scott Ave. about 2 p.m. to fight a fire in scrap lumber, believed set by boys. While the crew was out, another call five minutes later brought a second force of four men to a public housing dwelling at 418 Norfolk St., occupied by Shirley Menara. The men found a closet was ablaze.

The men pumped water on the blaze, which had moved into the ceiling and wall. Most of the loss was to wearing apparel and was estimated at $1,000.

The first crew returned to the station at 2:35 and the other at 3:10 p.m.

the house until someone came to repair and repaint the damaged bedroom. But, the most searing memory of this tragic event was that even though my mother could, at times, be a forceful fury to reckon with, she was utterly defenseless and dependent on us.

These signpost incidents throughout my childhood reminded me of how truly blessed I was to have my health—the ability to ride my bike, dance, and run.

Debbie enjoys a summer day in Ironwood, Michigan. 1971.

Girls Growing Up

My oldest sister, Debbie, was cool. She had cool friends, cool clothes, and an ultra-groovy, hippie-like attitude. While Madeline was impersonal and introverted, Debbie was a social butterfly with attitude. Both were responsible and hardworking, but their relationship with Mumma could not have been more different. Mumma had Madeline wrapped around her finger. But not Debbie.

It was 1968 when Debbie moved from Bessemer to Ironwood. The eleven-year-old girl went to work immediately as Mumma's caregiver. I was too little to do certain chores, and Debbie took the brunt of the more arduous tasks. When she went grocery shopping, she toted me along as she pulled the red wagon. Once, I was too tired to walk, and I climbed into the wagon, and she pulled me all the way up hilly Aurora Street. As Debbie hoisted me along, I took advantage of my free ride by thrusting out my hand and touching the daisies that grew along the curbside, making the ride that much more enjoyable.

Debbie was spreading her wings and testing her independence as she entered her teenage years. She'd come home after school, do her chores, and was right back out of the house with her friends. During this period, Madeline and I assumed more of the responsibilities of caring for Mumma and our home. By the time Debbie entered high school, her rebellious streak grew. She yearned for her independence and demanded it; as a result, she and Mumma argued.

I yearned for an active social life like Debbie, so in seventh grade, I tried out for cheerleading, but didn't make the team. I was crushed. I trudged inside the house and threw my books down. Mumma confided she knew the outcome. "But how?" "I called the school," she said matter-of-factly. "How could you do that?" I blurted out. She continued on and said she was only trying to help. But I saw it differently. She shouldn't have interfered.

I yelled. This uproar surprised not only my mother, but me. I never spoke back. She was momentarily quiet, then lamented, "I didn't mean to... I was just—" "You shouldn't have called," I blurted. I shook my head in disgust and marched off to the bedroom. As I sat on the bed, I grappled with guilt. I went to bed defeated that I didn't make the team and doubly defeated that I yelled at my mother. Never again did I raise my voice to her.

But not Debbie. Debbie was fiercely independent and let Mumma know in no uncertain terms. It didn't matter if Mumma said she couldn't go out. Debbie was going. Many a time, I ran from the room and covered my ears when they quarreled with each other. I was baffled at how Debbie could argue with Mumma. Once, I asked Debbie how she could yell at Mumma like that. Debbie shrugged, threw on her jacket, and was out the door.

Debbie's high school sweetheart, Frank Barbera, was a spunky, kind-hearted, charming, and good-looking Italian boy. Much like my dad, Debbie's boyfriend was soft-spoken, but more importantly, Mumma liked him. We all liked

Frank. He was a happy-go-lucky guy and often took us on car rides to Norrie Park to go swimming and then on a jaunt to Dairy Queen. More than once, Frank let me take a ride on his motorcycle with him. Other times we loaded up in the "pasty van" (his dad owned the popular, Joe's Pasty Shop), and he cranked up songs like "More Than a Feeling" from the rock group Boston, "Lady" by Styx, or the theme song to Hawaii Five-O. I felt so liberated jostling around the back of the van as we cruised along the roads of Ironwood. I know Johnny and Kelly especially enjoyed these excursions. Frank was cheerful and polite, and he was one of the few people Mumma didn't mind having in the house. Or, was it because she could keep an eye on Debbie?

Essentially, we kids were Mumma's eyes. Often, Debbie and Frank snuck off into the kitchen and made out. Of course, Madeline, Greg, and I bubbled over at the prospect of being tagged as make out session spies. We crouched, onto all fours, and snuck around the kitchen door, and scoped them out. I gawked at how intertwined their bodies were. Their faces were smooshed together like one big pancake. It looked to me like their tongues got a pretty good work out, all pressed up and roaming all over the place. Pretty regularly, they sucked at each other's necks, too. Why, I thought? What is the point? It didn't really matter. It was obvious they enjoyed each succulent moment. Every now and again, Mumma called me over to the couch. "Go see what they're doing." I crawled over to the kitchen, peeked around the fridge, and sure enough, like clockwork, they had their hands everywhere and lips locked. I crept over to Mumma and whispered, "They aren't doing anything, just reading a book." She wasn't buying it. She shook her head and waved me off.

Inevitably, after Frank left, Debbie tried to hide her hickies. Mumma knew better; they argued again, and then Debbie stormed off to the bedroom or out the door.

Once, Debbie showed me the hickey on her neck. She good-naturedly unwrapped the scarf around her neck and lifted it up so I could get a better look. It was all red and bruised. "Does it hurt?" She laughed at me, "No." "But Deb, it's all red and purple, and well, it has to hurt." She tossed a pillow at me, tied the scarf around her neck, pranced over to the closet, tossed off her clothes, and trotted around the room in her underwear and bra. She was comfortable in her body, and I was intrigued at how she confidently flaunted her femininity. In contrast, I was self-conscious and tried to cover up. But not Deb, she was a free spirit and comfortable with her sexuality. Years later, it dawned on me that Debbie's sexual independence and partying contributed to Mumma's anxiety.

For all of Debbie's rebellious teenage moments that agonized Mumma, she treated me with respect and I admired her. She was determined to remain a free spirit. By far, the greatest and most impactful influence Debbie had on me had to do with a flagpole. I was eleven years old, and my life would change forever.

Debbie cradles Peppy. Wendy peers behind the screen door, circa Summer 1974.

Greg and Wendy just joined the Squires Drum and Bugle Corps.
We proudly posed in our new uniforms. Shirley on couch.
Summer 1975.

A World Beyond Swing Sets and Trees

It was early summer. I was jumping rope at my favorite spot—the lilac bush. A car drove up, and Debbie jumped out. She was carrying a long silver pole with a flag. She nodded goodbye to her friend and started to wave the flagpole. Extraordinary magic floated through the Midwestern summer skies that afternoon.

I was completely enamored as she marched across the lawn while cleverly maneuvering the flag in various directions. Spellbound, I released the jump rope, letting it fall to the ground. The white, blue, and gold colors and sweeping movement of the silk as it billowed in the hot summer wind spirited me in an adventurous direction.

Debbie had become a member of the Blue Knights Jr. Drum and Bugle Corps. I peppered her with questions about the drum corps. Greg was interested as well, so he and I followed her to a rehearsal at the Memorial Building. We were enthralled with the bustle of activity of musicians and the color guard.

Because Greg and I were younger, we couldn't join the Blue Knights (the 'big' corps), but we could join the Squires (the small feeder corps). I couldn't decide if I wanted to play the horn, the drums, or carry a flag.

I wandered around the various rooms. David Veda, the drum major, was leading the horn players in warm-ups in a side room. Then I ambled outside and found the drummers practicing paradiddles at lightning speed.

While searching for Debbie I explored the Memorial Building. I meandered along the barren hallways, careful not to slip on the marble floors. I zigzagged up and down the flights of granite stairs taking a moment in the foyer to study the bronze, larger-than-life statue of a soldier carrying his gun. I peered in closed doors and as always marveled at the massive columns, arches, and beautiful stained-glass windows. Eventually, I made my way into the basement, past the swimming pool, and into the gymnasium where I found the color guard. I sat in the upper bleachers, engrossed with the routines that Cheri DeCarlo, the color guard captain, led them through. Studying them from afar, I was intrigued as they marched in various formations. The flags made a whooshing sound and the click and clack of the poles in the holsters was stimulating. I decided what I wanted to do in drum corps—be in the color guard.

Later that evening, Cheri ushered me off to the equipment room, placed a flag holster that had a small silver cup around my waist, and I joyfully waved the flag around. It was fun. But I was worried. On the way home, Greg and I lamented if Mumma would actually let us join. To our surprise, she did; not only because Debbie was part of the organization, but the managers (Charlotte and Joe DeCarlo) called our mother and assured her they would watch over us. Greg and I were official members of "The Squires." I brimmed with confidence when I tried on my uniform. It was a short, gold skirt, with a gold cummerbund, a blue bolero jacket, and a navy-blue sombrero hat.

What excited me even more was that Mumma allowed me to work as a busgirl at the very popular Friday night "Blue Knight's Fish Fry." Granted, I was eleven years old, but Mumma was confident that Joe and Charlotte would keep an eye on me. The DeCarlo family was especially kind and supportive to me throughout my years in the Blue Knights.

The "Big Parade" commemorating the U.P.'s American Legion and Ironwood Summerfest (aka Flag Day Parade) was the maiden parade in which I marched. While awaiting the ceremony, however, I had my first disappointment—I learned that I could not wear the same white ankle marching boots that Debbie wore in the Blue Knights. I fancied these boots, but instead, I had to settle for blue sneakers. I was not going to let this deter me. Determined, I saved up my money from tips and my newspaper route and picked the sneakers that best matched my Squire's uniform.

The day before the event, Greg and I were giddy beyond words. We barely slept all night. Greg and I had found a wholesome outlet. Drum corps replaced our frolicking, fantasy playtimes. We were growing up.

On the day of the parade, all the participants and marching units met at Ayer Street around the corner from Central School. It was a flurry of activity, colorful floats, high school marching bands, drill teams, drum and bugle corps, and Boy Scout and Girl Scout troops. As the groups lined up in their parade order, I took my position within the flag line. I stood straight and proud, and clutched tightly to the flagpole that was safely secured in my holster as the wind whipped the billowing silk cloth high above me. As we started down the parade route along Ayer to Lawrence Street to McLeod Street, the Squires drum corps turned the corner and exhilarating joy flooded over me. Crowds of people waving mini flags lined the streets. People cheered, clapped, smiled, and seemed to enjoy themselves. I was overcome with a sense of freedom that I had never experienced. I felt alive.

I belonged to a group with a common goal. As we marched along the street with other marching units and floats, the stimulation consumed me. I uncovered a wellspring of jubilation. A world beyond swing sets and trees. From this point forward, I dove wholeheartedly into the drum corps universe.

A year later, when I was twelve, I joined the big corps and proudly wore those white marching boots with honor. One benefit of marching with the Blue Knights was, not only did we march in local parades, we also performed in field competitions. During the summer months, we traveled locally to neighboring towns and competed with other drum corps at high school football stadiums. I found liberation when performing on the manicured, spacious football fields, and hearing the thunderous applause of the crowds from the stands. The stadium lights and the feeling of community with fellow drum corps performers illuminated something far greater than the arena—it filled a void in my heart.

If the parades and field competitions didn't satisfy my fervor, I was about to be mind-blown. Charlotte and Joe took an annual trip to a major drum corps show in Whitewater, Wisconsin. Much to our surprise, Mumma allowed

Greg and me to travel to lower Wisconsin. I assured her I would pay for everything. I squirreled away every tip from bussing and all the income from my newspaper route.

Debbie also assured Mumma she would watch out for us. But, of course, she didn't; Debbie was off having fun with her friends. It didn't matter. Greg and I were joined at the hip. We sat in the bleachers reveling in the performance of every drum corps at the stadium football field. In between performances, we roamed the back of the stadium visiting all the souvenir booths.

Never before had I heard or beheld such a glorious and bounteous cacophony of music and pageantry. The musical bravado of the horns' melodies and the drums' rhythms penetrated deep within my bones. The instrumental sounds soared and reverberated throughout the Whitewater, Wisconsin arena. The color guards were in perfect unison and symmetry as they tossed rifles and flags. It was as if a thousand fireworks went off inside me and were continually sizzling and crackling with delight. Quite simply, this drum corps show was overwhelmingly intoxicating.

By the time the Blue Devils and Madison Scouts entered the field and performed, I was beyond myself. I returned home from that drum corps show a different girl. From that point forward, I lived, breathed, and ate drum corps. I was what my dad referred to (in later years) as a "drum corps nut."

Mumma noticed the change, too. I was unable to contain my excitement after coming home from a parade or a competition. She listened to me go on and on about the different corps and the color of their uniforms, how loud the music sounded, how the rifles and flags moved in perfect unison, how incredibly fun it was to see all the people in the football stands. She was happy for me. In some ways, I presume our weekend trips in the drum corps activities were her eyes to the outside world she hadn't experienced since her late thirties.

While performing with the Squires, Blue Knights, Blue Stars from Wisconsin, and Blue Devils from California I formed some of the fondest memories, touring across the country, meeting people from all walks of life, and entertaining audiences. The drum corps activities provided social interaction, physical exercise with the marching and movement, and the ability to focus and gain strength during long rehearsal sessions on a football field in the middle of summer.

I look back at this period of my life now as an adult, and recognize that the drum corps activity gave me the opportunity to channel my energies and focus on situations other than the chaos that surrounded my family life. It sustained me through high school and when I initially moved to California.

In addition, I wonder if my yearning for independence and freedom worried Mumma. We were growing up. We couldn't take care of her forever, and I am sure she also considered who would take care of us when she died.

Unbeknownst to any of us, however, that time of reckoning would arrive sooner than imagined—little did any of us know that in one year, our mother would be dead.

When we first moved into our new house, Mumma was in
the bedroom. That lasted a short time before she migrated
into the living room. Left to right: Louie with his girlfriend,
Angie, prior to getting married. Johnny, Wendy, Ricky. On
floor, Kelly with our dog Peppy, and Greg with Frito, the bird.
December 1974.

Final Days

By 1977, we were comfortable with our living arrangements. My siblings and I were growing up and finding our
independence: Debbie and Frank were planning to marry;
Ricky had returned from prison; Madeline was steadfast in
her quest to become a nun; and Greg and I were consumed,
heart and soul, in drum corps.

Life went on. Then one day, it all changed.

I was washing dishes in the kitchen sink, and I heard
Mumma yell, "I told you not to do that!" I rushed out and
glanced around. "What, Mumma? What?" She had a blank
stare as she took a long drag from her cigarette. She turned
and scrutinized me, "What are you looking at?" It was as
if nothing happened. I thought it strange, but went back to
the kitchen and finished doing the dishes. But it was not a
one-time outburst. These random ramblings persisted, and
at a steadier pace. I was worried. My siblings were worried.
During these episodes, the things Mumma said were so
outrageous we just had to laugh; but right under the surface
of the laughter was a tangible fear that I had never experienced—what is happening with my mother?

One morning, three of us were in the kitchen when she
babbled loudly. None of us looked up.

"Now what is she talking about?" Greg muttered.

"Who knows?" Madeline said as she trotted out of
the room.

Greg and I glanced at each other with a worried look.

"She's crazy," I said.

"Don't say that," Greg argued.

"But what else is it? Why is she acting this way?" I was confused.

Another time, I was at the kitchen table and Mumma shouted, "Wendy, come here!" I sauntered into the living room and stood by her. "Sit next to me." I sat on the couch, and from out of nowhere she blurted, "Do you have sex?" Startled at this question, I tensed, thinking she was having one of her episodes. We never talked about sex in our family. Even when I had my first period, I quietly emerged out of the bathroom and in hushed tones uttered, "Mumma, I'm bleeding like you." Matter-of-factly, she said, "It's what women do."

She asked again, "Do you have sex?" I realized she was very serious and very coherent. "Of course I don't, Mumma. Why would you say that?" She muttered under her breath, then said, "Good, you shouldn't have sex. You're too young. It causes trouble, sex. Do you hear, do you hear me?" "Yes, Mumma, I do hear you," I assured her. "Good," she replied. "Stay away from those boys." I had no idea where this was coming from. It both frightened and worried me.

Before I could ask her anything, she grabbed my arm and scowled, "Look! You have scurf on your arm. You haven't cleaned up. Go clean up." I examined my arm and she was right, there was some dirt in my elbow crease. She pulled me closer and examined my neck. "Make sure you clean your neck, too. Go, go clean up."

This would be the last personal, coherent conversation I had with my mother.

Not long after this incident, I was giving Mumma the bedpan, and when I pulled it out from underneath her, I was bewildered at the sight of blood in the bedpan. I hadn't given her a Kotex for years, and it was obvious something wasn't right. It wasn't long after that episode she was taken to Grandview, the local county hospital in Ironwood. Little did we know this would be the last time she would be in her house with her children.

When Mumma was admitted to the hospital, Debbie was nineteen years old and could legally watch over the younger children for a short period of time while long-term plans were determined, and as a result they allowed us to stay together as a family unit. I visited Mumma as often as I could. Friends gave us rides to the hospital, and I spent hours by my mother's side after school and on the weekends.

During this period, I do not recall the word 'dementia' ever mentioned. We assumed she was going crazy or senile because of the MS, but she was never officially diagnosed with memory loss. It would be years later that it occurred to me that she might have had dementia. Because Mumma was usually too out of it to talk, I wandered around the hospital. I spent many an hour in the gift shop. I got to know the nurses and doctors, and everyone treated us kindly.

While Mumma was hospitalized at Grandview, we managed to live as normally as possible, given our mother was dying. Music took on a whole new meaning for me. During these final days, listening to drum corps albums and music on the radio was how I coped. I lost myself in the music

and the lyrics. I went to school, came home, did homework and my chores. But then, I encountered additional
information that agonized me to my core.

I had returned from the hospital after having spent a
good portion of the day with my mother. I was catching up
on homework. Madeline was in her bedroom singing, "How
Great Thou Art," for a solo she was going to sing at St.
Ambrose Catholic Church.

Greg slid into his seat at the kitchen table and sat across
from me. He was silent, and I peered up. He whispered,
"Wendy, I think we might be put up for adoption."

"What?" I was stunned.

He remained silent.

"What are you talking about?" I asked.

He shrugged. "Debbie mentioned it."

I threw my pencil down, shut my history book, dashed
down the hallway, and burst into Debbie's room as she was
applying her makeup.

"Debbie, Greg just said we might be adopted," I asked,
more a statement than a question.

"Shhh." She kept brushing her cheeks with the blush.

"Where'd you hear this?" I continued.

She shrugged. "Louie. It's not definite."

I plopped on the bed. "We can't be adopted. No way."

Greg entered the room and sat on the bed.

He concurred, "Debbie, you can watch us. You're old
enough. You're our big sister."

Debbie placed the brush on the dresser and turned
to us.

"Not long term," Debbie assured us.

"How about Louie? Ricky? They're old enough," I asked.

"They're talking to Dad," Debbie said.

"Who's talking to Dad?" I demanded.

"The State. They contacted him and are seeing if he'll take us in."

Greg and I glanced at each other. A sense of relief surged through me. But then, panic set in.

"But what if he doesn't? We can't be split up. No!" I protested.

"I don't think we have a choice, Wendy, we're wards of the State," Debbie reminded me.

We sat in silence. The full weight of this news enveloped me.

Not only was Mumma going to die; there was a strong possibility I would lose my brothers and sisters.

With this distressing piece of information weighing over me, I felt a deep sense of despair I had never felt up to this point. It was as if someone turned off the light switch, and in the murky twilight, I couldn't locate the switch to turn it back on. I lumbered in hazy, unending fog. And then the news arrived.

It was Palm Sunday, April 3, 1977. It lightly snowed the day before. It was a cloudy, chilly, early spring evening. I was staring out the front bedroom window while my siblings huddled on the bed and talked. As usual, our conversations were about our future. Would Mumma ever come home? If not, where would we live? Would we be adopted out? Would we lose each other?

We heard the front door open. We stopped talking. We heard soft footsteps on the wooden floor and then Agnes, who by now was more of a family friend than just a Social Services part-time caretaker, poked her head in. She didn't have to say anything. Her look said it all. A wave of anxiety washed over me when Debbie left the room and talked with Agnes. We were not prepared for the finality of our mother's death—no matter how many conversations we had on the subject over the years, we were in freefall without Mumma.

Now, what would happen?

I cried myself to sleep every night. I missed Mumma. I prayed to God that I could live with my brothers and sisters. The thought of being separated from my siblings was incomprehensibly too daunting for me to digest.

The Wooden Box

For all the countless conversations we had with our mother about her dying, nothing prepared me for the moment when I saw Mumma's lifeless body lying in the casket. It was a gut punch to the soul. During the evening funeral visitation, I experienced my second significant psychic encounter, the first being my childhood telekinetic incident when my grandmother passed away.

I walked into a dimly lit, spacious room filled with mingling grown-ups who spoke in hushed tones. Then I saw it—the wooden box! Flowers adorned both sides, and the shiny paneling of the casket shimmered under the lights. It was obvious why I was here, and I knew my mother was in that box, but I couldn't find the courage to approach the casket.

My brother Greg gently grabbed my hand and led me toward the front of the room. I peered down, and there she was, Mumma, wearing her favorite green dress that my sister Debbie chose for our mother's final appearance in this world. Her face was made up—she never wore make-up. She looked otherworldly. I scrutinized her weathered hands. No amount of makeup could hide the yellowed, smoke-stained fingertips. Her lips were shut tightly, pursed together, as if all her secrets, all her pain, all her memories were locked tightly inside and would go with her forever to the grave.

I wanted to crawl in the casket and lay beside her. Greg inched closer, and we momentarily glanced at each other. He was crying. I placed my hand on his, and we stood there pressed up against the casket, hanging on our mother's every feature: the light-colored wart above her lip, the lines in her face, her short, fine, dark hair. After a while, Greg shuffled off. I stood there. I couldn't move. It was as if my feet were glued to the floor. I skimmed my hands gently across the folds of her dress, her bony hands, her weathered face, her thin lips—taking in every last bit of her essence. This was it. The last time I would see her. These last moments with her in the casket were all I had left of my mother. I grasped the finality and acknowledged I had to say goodbye, but I couldn't. I wasn't ready.

An avalanche of desolation descended upon me. The grieving sensation was unbearable. A whirlwind of emotions consumed me. A knife was wedged in my heart. It was as if someone popped a balloon, and all the air went out from me.

I stumbled backward—to the back of the room. I huddled close to a dark-brown wooden wall, at a distance from the people, the noise, and the casket. I was emotionally glued to that wall; it was my anchor and my support. I clenched my hands together. I fiddled with my mother's diamond ring. After Mumma died Debbie came into the bedroom one evening and sat on the bed next to me. She held out the ring, "Mumma said it was yours." I reached out my hand and she placed the gem in my palm. We spent a moment in silence. The reality of our mother's death blanketed us both in melancholy. And now, here I was at my mother's visitation. The diamond ring was all I had left of her. The trickle of tears broke like a fractured glacier that could no longer stand firm. The innermost crevice of my being burst open. It was as if I was plunged into the depths of the ocean.

In between the gasps for air and the sobbing, my body started to tremble. Suddenly, the room was engulfed in blazing light—as if someone just ripped the roof off the building and the sun's penetrating rays cut through the core of the room.

Sounds were hushed, muffled, and then quieted. I found myself rising slowly but surely out of my body like a helium-filled balloon. I steadily floated above my body until I was safely tucked in the opposite corner of the room. It was as if I was an invisible girl caressed and lifted to safety by an invisible hand. The pain was no longer consuming me. I felt calm, serene, and sheltered.

While in this state, I took note of people in the room and the casket, but I was more focused on my body. It was crystal clear that I wasn't my physical body. I was beyond the bounds of the physical world. I was an animated twinkle of light. There was no past, no present, no fear, and no death. I was the tranquil eye of a hurricane—calm in the midst of calamity.

Etched in my memory was my grief-stricken body pinned against the wall, sobbing uncontrollably. I wanted to reach out to Wendy and tell her, "It's okay. Mumma went to a good place." But I could only observe my physical body and allow her to wail in a giant sea-swell of tears.

Time had no meaning. I was a spectator observing my adolescent body bawling. Then, as quickly as this out-of-body experience began, I gently slipped back into my body. The crying subsided, and I scanned the room. Did anyone know where I went? Did they notice me floating above the room? It didn't seem so. A woman approached and gently placed her hands on my shoulders, and I allowed the full weight of my body to fall against her.

Shortly afterwards, I was outside the funeral home. Night skies were descending. The air was crisp; snow scattered on the ground. Winter melting into spring. My body felt tingly, and the fresh air felt pleasant against my skin. A tree caught my eye—a tall, resilient, solid maple tree. Leafless. Barren. I contemplated climbing the tree, but there were no leaves, nowhere to hide, and besides, it was too chilly to climb in my dress.

I gazed up at the sky and wondered where Mumma was. It was obvious it was only a shell of a woman in the casket, but where did her spirit go? Many a time when I was younger, my siblings and I laid on the fresh summer grass under a nighttime star-filled sky and named the stars and the constellations. We believed that when people died, they transformed into a heavenly star. When a star twinkled, we imagined they were waving to us. Could one of those stars be Mumma—that starlight of twinkle high up in the heavens waving to me at this very moment?

All those years, Mumma was preparing me for this day. After her lengthy illness, the day had arrived—it was final. Though Mumma was gone, I recognized somewhere from deep inside my being that it would be okay. I would be okay. It would have to be. I had no choice. I had to keep it together and go on. That is what she would have wanted, and I wanted to make my mother proud.

Left to right: Shirley (Mumma), Glen aka Bobbie (Gramps), Josie (Grandma), Louie (Dad), Allen (my mother's brother). Milwaukee, Wisconsin. May 18, 1951.

Secrets of Shame

As devastated as I was by the death of my mother, nothing could have prepared me for the scandals that were revealed shortly after my mother's body was buried deep in the ground, and her spirit was unencumbered on the other side.

Perhaps this is the core reason that I wrote this memoir— to unleash the shackles of shame that held my mother in her unholy mental bondage while on earth.

Times were different then, compared to the present time while writing this book, but shame is shame, and shame runs deep. People's secrets can go with them to their graves, never making peace or finding the healing for which they deeply yearned while embodied. The guilt-ridden scars of regret, shame, and remorse lay hidden in darkened closets awaiting their discovery—at last freeing the burdened soul.

❦ ❦ ❦

I was now in eighth grade and Greg and I were more tightly bonded than ever. "Evergreen" (the love theme from *A Star is Born*) was in regular rotation on the radio. This song comforted me following the passing of my mother. Each and every time I heard the opening notes play, they transported me into a sanctuary of peace. I was listening to the song on the radio thinking about Mumma when Greg sauntered into the bedroom and asked, "Wanna go to Mumma's grave?" I clicked off the radio and dashed from the room.

It was a dreary, ominous, late summer afternoon. Thunderstorms were brewing. We hopped on our bikes and rode the mile or so to Riverside Cemetery. We visited our grandmother's grave first then headed over to Mumma's plot of land. At the time, we had no money for a gravestone, so the modest, silver grave marker was all that stood at her plot of dirt.

We prayed, and then felt the need to have a piece of Mumma with us. And so—we stole the grave marker. Greg yanked the makeshift headstone from the ground and held it toward me. I blurted, "No, we'll get punished!" He chuckled, shoved the marker inside the front of his jacket, and jumped on his bike. I quickly mounted my bike and followed him out of the cemetery.

On the way home, the rain clouds parted, and the thunder struck. I yelled through the torrential downpour and lightning, "Greg. I told you, God's punishing us!" He rode on ahead as I scrutinized the crackling heavens, expecting a lightning bolt to strike us down.

We entered the house dripping wet and snuck into the front bedroom. We plopped on the bed, and stared at the dirt-laden marker bearing our mother's name, "Shirley Ann Morrison February 13, 1931–April 3, 1977."

The First Secret

My dad was a generous man. He was a second-generation Italian. His parents, John and Alice, came from Vicenza, a city in northeastern Italy in 1914, and initially lived in South Dakota before moving on to New York, then California, and finally settling in Hurley, Wisconsin in 1922. Dad frequently reminded us, "The name matters." He was proud of the Menara name. He often reminded me, as he smoked his pipe and worked his crossword puzzles with his thick glasses low on the bridge of his nose, that it was an uncommon Italian name that meant "axe." I was proud of my name. I was proud to be an Irish-, Chippewa-, Italian-blooded girl from Ironwood, Michigan.

But that pride would soon be dashed.

Mumma and Dad were married in July 1949. During this period in our country, it was absolutely socially unacceptable to be pregnant and not married—a *'Scarlet Letter'* mentality. Right out of high school, my mother married my dad. Prior to meeting my mother, Dad was a World War II veteran who served with the Third Infantry of the Rock of the Marnez Division of the Seventh Army. It was the top-honored division of the Second World War, having received more honors than any infantry division. He was wounded while fighting both in France and in Germany. He was ultimately awarded the Purple Heart with Oak Leaf Cluster for meritorious service. He was also awarded the Bronze Star for acts of bravery.

Upon returning home from the war, Dad was injured in a blast accident in the Ironton Mine in the Spring of 1948. He lost one eye and suffered multiple punctures of the other eyeball, which destroyed his vision. Hope was renewed when it was revealed that he could distinguish the presence of objects. The town of Bessemer held a charity baseball event and the proceeds were given to my dad to visit Johns Hopkins Hospital for delicate eye surgery.

Because time was of the essence, the honeymoon was short-lived. Dad traveled to Maryland for the eye surgery while Mumma stayed home in Michigan, expectant with her first child. Dad returned home with a reasonably functioning, working eye. Over the years, he worked at the post office part time, he owned a clothing store and a grocery store, while Mumma stayed home. But there were cracks in this marriage that only my older brothers, Louie and Ricky, were privy to; information that was revealed to me only after my mother died.

After her death, five children were still in school. We were informed that, instead of going to foster care, our dad would move from the town of Bessemer to care for the remaining children until we graduated. He made it clear that as soon as the last child was out of school, he was moving back to his treasured town of Bessemer.

Dad, Louie Sr., works his crossword puzzle.

This was fine with me. I planned to move to California as soon as I graduated high school. What mattered most was not only was I able to maintain living with my brothers and sisters, but my wish to live with my dad was now a full-fledged reality. I settled into my ninth-grade year feeling confident. Then the walls fell in.

❦ ❦ ❦

It was a hot, sunny afternoon when the first guarded family secret presented itself. This soon-to-be-uncovered revelation about my mother would have a life-altering effect on me.

Relatives and friends mingled, perhaps sharing scandals my mother had trusted were buried with her. I do not recall what the gathering was for, but what I do remember, and it is forever seared upon my brain, are these words:

"Did you hear? Dad isn't our real dad. We all have different fathers."

As the words tumbled out of my brother's mouth, the sun appeared hotter. The rays scorched at the deepest chambers of my soul. I turned from my brother and wandered off to a nearby grove of white birch trees. I let my body collapse on the ground beside the white peeling trunk as the full weight of this piece of information engulfed me and oozed into the depths of my subconscious.

The sky shattered into a million pieces. My identity fractured. Did I even know my mother? So many questions I wanted to ask her. The answers went with her at her death. My core splintered and shredded as I processed the information. Who was my real dad then? These aren't my true brothers and sisters? What nationalities am I? Why didn't Mumma tell us? I refused to accept this revelation about my mother.

From that point forward, every conversation with Dad, no matter how casual it started—how was basketball practice, what was for dinner, what was the forecast for tomorrow's weather—ended with me asking about Mumma. I didn't let it go. Like a rabid dog with a bone— I needed to know. Dad shared a great deal of information. He divulged that she was a heavy drinker who had affairs throughout their marriage. Louie (the oldest child) was his only biological child. The others—well, the others were fathered by other men. He candidly shared private information about his and Mumma's love life, including the fact that throughout it all, he continued to love her. Dad maintained Mumma got MS from all her drinking. He stood by his opinion. I appreciated that he was honest and forthcoming.

I had to process this newly revealed information that my dad shared:

She was a cruel woman with a temper. *Yes, I saw how she treated us, and especially Kelly and Madeline.*

She drank. *How could that be? We never had alcohol in the house. I clearly remember her yelling at Ricky about drinking.*

She had numerous affairs during the marriage. *Is that why she told me sex was bad and to stay away from the boys? Is that why she hounded Debbie all the time?*

Now that this skeleton was free and unfettered, my siblings and I barraged Dad with questions. He was exceedingly patient and did his best to answer each and every endless question. There were certain questions that demanded answers, and we asked the questions a trillion times.

Who were the men? *He was familiar with some of the men she was with, but wasn't sure precisely who fathered whom. He could only conjecture on who laid sperm in my mother's womb.*

When did the cheating start? *The extra-marital affairs started soon after their marriage.*

Why? *He had no answer for the why.*

My siblings and I spent the rest of our lives trying to piece together and find these men who impregnated and then discarded our mother, and ultimately left our dad to provide for the children they abandoned.

My dad wasn't perfect (what parent is?), but he was noble to sacrifice and move from his residence to another city and be responsible for children he never fathered. He often revealed the reason he stayed with my mother all those years was that he didn't feel the children should be without a father in the home while she was out wandering. But even the staunchest and most patient of human beings has a breaking point; and my father reached the end of his rope. Before Kelly and I were born, he filed for divorce. But that didn't stop my mother. Her habitual promiscuity continued until MS took hold of her. He also confided that the reason he moved to Ironwood after her death was that he believed the children should remain together and graduate from our current school and not disrupt our lives any more than they already had been.

During the research of this book, I uncovered information that my dad, indeed, did leave my mother. Mumma was at least truthful about that segment of the story. I reckon after all of the quarrels, her drunken wanderings, philandering escapades, he had had enough. They separated in early October 1962. Shortly after the separation, Mumma became pregnant with me. Five months before I was born, Dad filed for divorce in March 1963, citing adultery and repeated acts of extreme cruel and unusual punishment.

Dad (Louie Sr.) with seven of the children in Bessemer. After the divorce. Kelly and I were with our grandparents, Johnny was at Newberry State Hospital.

Left to right. Louie Jr., Ricky, Dad, Madeline, Greg, Debbie, Randy, and Jeff. Shirley was most likely in the hospital, at the beginning stages of her diagnosis with multiple sclerosis. Late 1960s.

After Dad confirmed that he, in fact, was not my biological father, a heavy, oppressive, cloud of shame hung over me. I was ashamed of my mother and my family name. I did my best to bury it and try to forget about it. School and drum corps continued to sustain me.

In my senior year, I was one of a few students who, because of excellent academic standing, was given an opportunity to get some real-life work experience in lieu of last-period class. The place where I worked was The Friend of the Court, at the Gogebic County Court House. While working there, I grew familiar with some cases and saw firsthand how heartbreaking and atrocious some family situations were. I had no idea that our own Menara family had its own thick file brimming with testimony from social workers that I unearthed during my research.

The Friend of the Court documents only solidified our family problems:

File No. 27
5th day of July, 1963
"They have learned and determined that said Shirley Ann Menara is neglecting the care and needs of said children, and is not providing them with proper care, maintenance, and upbringing, all of which is jeopardizing the welfare of said children. And has on various occasions abandoned said children to leave them to shift for themselves...Bureau of Social Aid advised me that...(Shirley) abandoned said children on Tuesday, July 2, 1963 and has not as yet returned to home.

7th day of May, 1964

"The son, Louis Jr., has had to shoulder much respon-sibility for the family care and supervision and he is quite mature in this regard, for his years. This is not, however, entirely fair to him, but it is a necessity. There is no question that at present the supervision of these children by the Probate Court should be continued for the best interests of the children. It is possible that foster home placement or adoption should, however, be considered...On the whole, it is a difficult situation at best."

While the divorce judgment was moving through the court system, my mother was pregnant with me. Con-sequently, only eight children were named on the final judgment. When I was eventually born in 1963, an Amended Divorce Judgment occurred on October 19, 1964. With it, nine siblings were now placed under the care and supervision of the Probate Court for Gogebic County. But what about the tenth child?

As I continued to study these court documents, I puzzled over why there wasn't an amendment when Kelly was born. While digesting the information presented within these documents, I realized that perhaps Mumma directed all her rage, her shame, on Kelly. The final child born would endure the brunt of all her past transgressions.

All of this information was in the public records. All of those unspoken truths, hidden between the lines, staring at me from the pages.

The Second Secret

My mother's skeletons continued tumbling out of the closet after her death. These unveilings contradicted the modest, helpless, bedridden mother I had known.

My brother Johnny wasn't born with a physical or mental disability. I learned that while Dad travelled for work one weekend, Mumma went on a drinking binge and abandoned my older brothers alone in the house. Johnny was just a baby. On this particular weekend, the heat went out. During the frigid, sub-zero temperatures in the dead of winter, Johnny contracted pneumonia, which, due to his high fever and subsequent stroke, led to his disability. I can only imagine the guilt and shame she bore, knowing that she caused her son's lifelong issues of mental and physical disabilities.

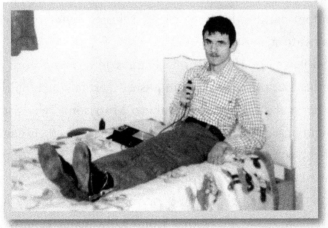

Johnny in the bedroom recording himself talking into the cassette recorder. This was one of his favorite pastimes. His left arm was slightly paralyzed and he wore a brace on his left leg, circa 1975.

The Third Secret

In my thirteenth year, I tumbled down a labyrinth of another heartbreaking, gut-wrenching truth:

Josephine, the grandmother I loved dearly, the grand-mother who cooked me Cream of Wheat and let me play in her lush garden, was in fact, not my biological grandmother. She was my great-aunt.

Imagine two sisters. One is a homebody, suffering in silence at her inability to conceive a child she and her husband desperately want. The other is loose, carefree, and wild.

The carefree sister gets pregnant. She's not married. Her philandering lumberjack of a boyfriend, Joseph Dillon, wants nothing to do with her. And, because of societal pressures, she has to give away her child—to her sister—the one who cannot have kids. No records, no messy paperwork, just a handover of her newborn child in some random parking lot on a frigid, February wintery day in Wauwatosa, Wisconsin.

So it was in 1931. Ruthie Francis Jones, who bore my mother out of wedlock, relinquished her daughter, Shirley, to her childless sister, Josephine Morrison. Two sisters bound in secrecy, the fate of my mother held in their hands. A baby given up at birth to the mother's sister. The adoption was never legalized. Shirley Dillon (as it was listed on the birth certificate) who will be forever known as Shirley Ann Morrison made the move from Milwaukee County to Gogebic County and assumed her new name and new family.

Even as a child, I always thought that Ruthie and Mumma looked similar. They both had the same dark hair, high cheekbones, shrewd, dark, penetrating eyes, thin lips, and small-framed bodies. Mumma was cheery when 'Aunt Ruthie' visited. The two women smoked cigarettes and talked about everything from the weather, to gossip about the relatives—everything but that fortified 'secret.' I wonder, as Mumma shooed me away and directed me to the bedroom, did they quietly share mother-and-daughter moments in between those drags of cigarettes?

৯৵ ৯৵ ৯৵

Mumma, why didn't you tell us? I only wish you had felt safe to share these burdensome secrets. I wonder if you had a friend to confide in, those moments when you were alone with your thoughts. I suppose alcohol was your friend until it was no more. I wish you would have talked to me. I would have listened. I would have done my best to understand and comfort you. Yet, I suppose it is too much to ask that anyone (especially a parent) share such intimate, uncomfortable truths with their child; perhaps I do not need to understand. Only accept. Time to turn the page.

Two sisters, Josephine and Ruthie. Boy unknown, circa 1950s.

Josephine holds her new baby girl, my mother, Shirley. This photo was likely taken after my mother was handed off from one sister to the other. My mother would now be known as Shirley Ann Morrison. The adoption was never legalized between the sisters. Spring 1931.

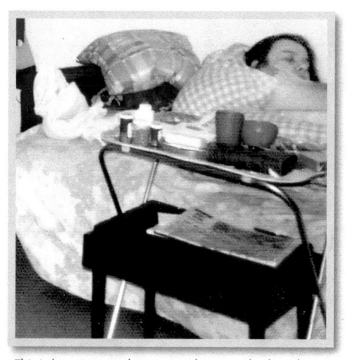

This is how I remember my mother—perched on the green couch. Nearby was the TV tray with her assortment of medicines, cigarettes, coffee, and newspaper. Summer 1975.

The Green Couch

The dark-green couch was the hub and core of our family's conversations. Even though Mumma bunked in the bedroom for a short while, it was the green couch from which she perched and controlled the family unit. It was on the green couch where Mumma inadvertently disclosed being called a bastard.

When I think back at the look of humiliation on my mother's face after she shared her intimate childhood experience, I believe she realized she had revealed too much information to me. My mother was damaged long before her illness began to decimate her body. Vulnerable. Desperate. Complex. She was deeply burdened by her own demons, unable to deal with her childhood tragedies. I wonder if perhaps the disease and medicines exacerbated or magnified her already volatile nature. I believe she did the best she could.

Mumma was a striking beauty in her younger years. The illness had to have obliterated her self-image. She was a proud woman, yet ashamed of her childhood and embarrassed by what had become of her once vibrant, healthy self. She went to her grave with her regrets. I wish she could have realized that she gifted the world ten beautiful children. A gift that will be shared for generations and beyond.

How do we cope with the dysfunction and traumas of our childhood? I perpetually asked these weighty questions when I was a child. I dug deep into the 'whys' of everything for as long as I can remember. As an adult, I contemplated how one copes with deep shame. How secrets can eat us alive and paralyze us mentally, emotionally, spiritually, and perhaps, even physically.

Looking back at my childhood fraught with adversity and chaos, my coping mechanism was to fully immerse myself in school activities and drum corps.

When I moved to California, I came to realize the quest to relocate from Michigan was more than just a life-long dream; it ultimately gave me freedom to leave behind shattered images of myself and my mother. The move to the West Coast was my escape.

It was agonizing that my mother's death left an indelible mark on my selfhood. But when the version of the mother I thought I knew collided with the reality of what I learned after her death—well, it was frankly, soul shattering.

It is hard enough to lose your mother as a young teenager, but to abruptly discover suppressed scandals seemed incomprehensible. I couldn't connect the dots. There was a short in the wire and no matter how I tried to tape the tattered ends and twist the wires together, things kept shorting out in my mind.

The move from Ironwood turned out to be my means of putting distance between myself and my childhood, thereby giving me a comprehensive way of coping. I needed this space to sort things out. I placed my family (relationships with siblings) on a prolonged and extended pause to find myself. I withdrew inward and immersed myself in metaphysical studies, meditation, and hypnotherapy.

Through years of spiritual studies, I recognized that the image I had of my mother was delicate. And when, as a child, I discovered she was primarily a drunken whore and was seen as such by my father and her friends, it demolished the image I had of her. I was confused, ashamed, and angry. I felt betrayed by her. We saw our mother in her utmost vulnerable state. Why didn't she tell us we had different fathers? But then perhaps she felt betrayed by her own biological mother handing her over to her sister. It took me years to heal the image of her—and of myself—to find peace and regain a solid foundation for myself.

I've come to realize that families come broken, some more fractured than others. For all that my family and I endured and experienced, we took responsibility in our own individual ways, dealt with the trauma, and made a life for ourselves—and we turned out okay. Even though only five of the ten siblings are alive at the writing of this book, we went on to have successful lives and loving families.

I was pleased to discover that, while Madeline didn't enter the convent, she had a great career in the military and was a pillar of support for her community prior to her death. Johnny succumbed to his life-long illness and died when he was in his early thirties. Ricky and Greg also passed away in their thirties, while Randy departed just shy of his fiftieth birthday. Debbie and Frank have two beautiful daughters. Louie and his family, along with my brother

Jeff, kept their roots in the Midwest, where they have a full and content life. My dad, true to his word, returned to his beloved town of Bessemer where he spent his final days.

Years later, when I had gained strength within myself, I started to open the doors to my siblings, I spoke with Kelly on the phone. At the end of the conversation, I asked, "How are you doing, Kelly? Considering, you know, what you went through as a kid—the abuse?" He was quiet for a moment and then whispered, "I have never hit my children, Wendy." I said, "I am glad to know you found healing, Kelly."

I hung up the phone. I rested back on the couch for a moment while a flood of tears washed over me. The smell of the bedpan, the sounds of Kelly screaming, the sight of Mumma in the coffin. Distant, healed memories. I was proud of my brother. He could have easily perpetuated what had been done to him. Instead, he figured out how to transmute that pain and focused his energies to contribute and be a productive member of society with a loving wife and family.

To me, he exemplifies the truth that, no matter how troubling your childhood may be, we have a choice. The last-born child—the one that suffered horrible abuse—the one who never made it into the final court documents as a Menara child—he did it—he rose above his turbulent childhood, broke the cycle of abuse, and thrived.

🐝🐝🐝

I couldn't have written this memoir even ten years ago; but after having read Hope Edelman's book *Motherless Daughters*, I realized that in order for me to move forward and to honor my mother's memory, I needed to acknowledge the full, unabridged life of my mother for the short time she was with me on earth.

"But every human relationship is affected by ambivalence, every mother an amalgam of the good and the bad. To mourn a mother fully, we have to look back and acknowledge the flip sides of perfection and love. Without this, we remember our mothers as only half of what they were, and we end up trying to mourn someone who simply didn't exist . . . I couldn't mourn my mother until I was ready to allow her, after death, to be nothing less—and nothing more—than she had been in life. If I can't mourn the Bad Mother, a piece of me remains forever connected to the piece of her I refuse to see."

—Hope Edelman

Leave the memory on the page
For those who shall come after
Words set ablaze the darkness
Illuminating the road ahead
Wendy J. Menara

Acknowledgments

It takes a robust group of people to release a book. While wordsmithing during the final editing phase, I stumbled upon a cool website, www.wordhippo.com. I call it a thesaurus on steroids. How many ways can I thank those who have offered encouragement, support, and assistance during the writing of this childhood memoir without using the word "thank." Allow me to put wordhippo.com to good use.

First shout-out—Anne Lamott. One of the first writing books I read was *Bird by Bird*. Her imaginative sentiment about embracing "shitty first drafts" has both impressed and inspired me throughout my storytelling life. With that said, a second shout-out to Charlene Burgi for reading those shitty first drafts before my stories were ready for public consumption.

Trang Bach
I always hold your opinion in high regard and welcomed your observations and commentary on the cover art and title possibilities.

Charisse Beronilla and Sergio Paganelli
The insight you provided on various aspects of the book as it moved through production were invaluable. Little details make the difference.

Charlene Burgi

Soul sister. The ultimate pillar of strength and support. You have been with me on this memoir journey from the beginning. When I found myself in a quandary and needed a sounding board you were there. I will be eternally grateful to you for being my champion and confidante, and for the countless hours you spent helping me navigate the telling of my childhood story. You are the most patient, kind, and loving person I know. Eternally humbled and honored to call you my friend.

Madison Butz, Development Manager at the National Multiple Sclerosis Society
I appreciate the invaluable input and information you provided. www.nationalmssociety.org

Bryan Cohen, CEO of Best Page Forward
I praise your sensational marketing copy and the patience you demonstrated as we sifted through multiple drafts. www.bestpageforward.net

Nancy Fish, Book Passage, Corte Madera, CA
You are the foundation of the Path-to-Publishing Program. No matter how many emails I sent, you always offered spot-on advice and a wealth of information. www.bookpassage.com

Jo Haraf

An accomplished writer, researcher, editor, and overall just a rock-solid, kind-hearted, and generous person. I appreciate your continued support and your time to read a draft of the memoir.

Elizabeth Holland
Intelligent, witty, compassionate. I knew when I started this memoir that I needed to have you as a beta reader. I value your attentiveness and nonjudgmental attitude.

Nadia Fletcher and Gary Kappel
"What do you think of this title? What about this cover? How does this sound? Are you sure?" Please know that your input was extremely helpful as I waded through various aspects during the creation of this book.

Gogebic County Clerk's Office
A special nod to the helpful staff.

Arnetta Jackson, Line Upon Line Services
Your meticulous attention to detail, reliable and sound advice while line editing and proofreading has allowed me peace of mind through this entire process. I am forever grateful. www.lineuponlineservices.com

Nathaniel Lagalo, Title Examiner, Associated Title & Closing Services Agency, Inc., Ironwood, MI
Special acknowledgments for providing valuable information during the research phase of the project.

Jean Mansen
Editor extraordinaire. Having you on this journey with me has made all the difference. Wordhippo cannot provide enough synonyms to fully convey my sincerest and heartfelt universal appreciation for your guidance, keen eye, understanding, caring, wise perspective, and your wicked sense of humor. You nudged me along with

utmost kindness and encouraged me to dig deeper with
each edit. I am amazed by your exceptional talent and
your gift of empathy. I think the world of you.
www.jeanmansen.com

Diane Meyer
You have been a long-time writing colleague. I cherish the
reassurance you continually provide and your eagerness
to read an early draft of the memoir.

Mary Muehlenbruch (Mary Cornelison Photography) and
Ralph Muehlenbruch, Vacaville, CA
For your creative eye and stellar patience while scanning
photos, performing color density and retouching, I shall
forever be obliged.

Andrew Kuula
11th-hour angel of authors.

Joanne Osterberg
Long-time friend and stupendous artist. Your artistic
talents continually amaze me, and your friendship is
deeper than the Piscean ocean.

Joanna Penn
The information you provided in your books and on your
website are a gold mine of reliable publishing advice and
referrals. www.thecreativepenn.com

Jim Shubin

Book designer of book designers. Your inquisitive and expressive self was a constant source of inspiration. I appreciate your patience. I applaud the tremendous creative contribution you made to this project.
www.bookalchemist.net

Chris Spitale

Marketing genius and whiz with words—you rock.

Mardel Taguinod

I respect the fact you listened to me ramble on and on about an assortment of elements of the book during our dog strolls around the neighborhood. I also recognize the numerous hours you spent reading several drafts of the memoir. Your optimistic outlook on the world inspires me.

Kenneth Wegmeyer

Oh, so many years ago in Ironwood, Michigan, you made your rounds as a Social Services worker. You have absolutely no idea (or maybe you do) how your visits to our house on McLeod street were a bright, golden, shiny spot in my day. I hold you in high esteem!

Becca Wolff, Berkeley City College

A remarkable screenwriting teacher. You assigned us to write a personal essay. And you imparted to your students that appealing stories have their roots in a deep, emotional connection with the author. At the time, I didn't realize

what an impact that writing assignment would have—but it most assuredly influenced me. It was the springboard that motivated me to write this memoir.
www.berkeleycitycollege.edu

Newspapers.com
A storehouse of research material.

Debbie Menara Barbera
Uber cool sister who dug through boxes and bags of photos and unearthed some gems. Yeah, I most definitely owe you a bottle (or maybe even a case) of wine.

Debbie, Jeff, Kelly, Louie
We are the last five standing of the ten Menara kids. Wonder how many more years we'll be around? For however long, may we experience love, contentment, compassion, awareness, wonder, and enthusiasm. May we embrace and express our fullest heavenly potential and talents all the days of our lives.

Cecil, the Super Dog
I must pay tribute to my canine companion and chairside scribe. This precious pooch who was abandoned on the streets of Fresno, California has brought joy to my life and, as a result, has helped heal many childhood wounds. She has spent hundreds of hours nestled by my side as I traveled through the pages of my childhood.

The Author

Following her childhood dream to live in California, Wendy J. Menara packed her suitcase immediately after high school and migrated West. Despite not knowing anyone, she settled in comfortably and made a home for herself in the San Francisco Bay area.

She worked in production for the film and TV industry and has had several scripts produced for stage and screen.

Wendy currently resides in the Sacramento Valley with her rescue dog Cecil.

Her debut book, *SILENCE OF SHAME: A Child Caring for Her Bedridden Mother* chronicles her chaotic childhood up until her mother's death.

www.wendyjmenara.com